Albert Camus,

Jean Sénac

or the Rebel Son

Albert Camus,

Jean Sénac

or the Rebel Son

/ HAMID NACER-KHODJA // TRANSLATED BY KAI KRIENKE /

Michigan State University Press / East Lansing

MICHIGAN STATE UNIVERSITY PRESS
East Lansing, Michigan 48823-5245

Printed and bound in the United States of America.

28 27 26 25 24 23 22 21 20 19   1 2 3 4 5 6 7 8 9 10

LIBRARY OF CONGRESS CATALOGING-IN-PUBLICATION DATA
Names: Nacer-Khodja, Hamid, author. | Krienke, Kai, translator.
Title: Albert Camus, Jean Senac or the rebel son / Hamid Nacer-Khodja ; translated by Kai Krienke.
Other titles: Albert Camus, Jean Senac, ou le fils rebelle. English
Description: East Lansing : Michigan State University Press, 2018.
| Series: African humanities and the arts | Includes bibliographical references.
Identifiers: LCCN 2018035320| ISBN 9781611863178 (pbk. : alk. paper) | ISBN 9781609175962 (pdf)
| ISBN 9781628953626 (epub) | ISBN 9781628963632 (kindle)
Subjects: LCSH: Camus, Albert, 1913–1960—Friends and associates. | Senac, Jean, 1926–1973—
Friends and associates. | Authors, Algerian—20th century—Biography. | Authors, French—20th century—
Biography. | Camus, Albert, 1913–1960—Correspondence. | Senac, Jean, 1926–1973—Correspondence.
Classification: LCC PQ2605.A3734 Z7218313 2018 | DDC 848/.91409 [B]—
dc23 LC record available at https://lccn.loc.gov/2018035320

Book design by Charlie Sharp, Sharp Designs, East Lansing, MI
Cover art and design by Hamid Tibouchi

Michigan State University Press is a member of the Green Press Initiative and is committed to developing
and encouraging ecologically responsible publishing practices. For more information about the Green
Press Initiative and the use of recycled paper in book publishing, please visit www.greenpressinitiative.org.

Visit Michigan State University Press at *www.msupress.org*

Contents

vii   Foreword *by Guy Dugas*

xiii   Preface by the Translator

xxi   Introduction

PART I. From a Literary Father to an Impossible Father (1947–1954)

3   CHAPTER 1. Birth of a Friendship

15   CHAPTER 2. Algerianism or *École d'Alger*

21   CHAPTER 3. The Son Faces the Father

31   CHAPTER 4. Towards a Political Literature

PART II. Literature between Rebellion and Revolution (1954–1958)

41   CHAPTER 5. November 1954: The "Just" Fight or Terrorism?

51   CHAPTER 6. The Civil Truce

61   CHAPTER 7. From a Literature of Combat to the Nobel Prize

83   CHAPTER 8. Sénac, Reader of Camus

89   Conclusion

PART III. Correspondence and Radio Shows

95   Jean Sénac and Albert Camus's Correspondence

131   Two Shows from Radio Algeria, Produced by Jean Sénac

141   Notes

173   Bibliography

Foreword

Guy Dugas

hat better way to honor an academic, after expressing admiration and esteem, than to further his work, to value his research, to strive for its dissemination, to clarify it, sometimes to question it, since in our field nothing is definitive and every discovery brings new ones. The accomplished scholar in literature and in social sciences isn't he who pretends to have an answer (what truth anyway in these fields?), but he who opens new roads and encourages new research through his writings.

It is mostly thanks to Hamid Nacer-Khodja that we have discovered the vast poetic, prosaic, and critical work of Jean Sénac. After his thesis, *Jean Sénac, critique algérien* [Jean Sénac, an Algerian critic], recently published in Algeria (Algiers: El Kalima, 2013), Hamid dedicated two essays to the Franco-Algerian writer and edited several of his poetry collections.

Already translated into Arabic, the essay presented here, *Albert Camus, Jean Sénac, or the Rebel Son*, was first published in 2004. Written from the partially unpublished correspondence between the two men, it appeared in a context of quasi-complete ignorance with respect to the artistic and political positions of the young Sénac from 1945 to 1955. It represented at the time an essential and reliable tool to measure not only the respective positions of two major actors faced with colonialism and Algeria's growing demands, but also the central role that Camus played for the generation of young intellectuals of all stripes that he patronized.

Many documents and correspondence have appeared for the past fifteen years—particularly since 2013, the year of Camus's centennial—that helped refine and broaden the topic. Which is what I hope to do here for this new edition.

. . .

It's a story of men—a beautiful and solemn tale of friendship between two men true to their own nature, with common backgrounds, who share the same illness (they suffer from tuberculosis) and the same passions.

Already a well-known writer, Camus left his native land for the capital, where he made a name for himself in the world of journalism and publishing. A charismatic figure, admired by his fellow Algerians, Camus directs the "Espoir" collection with Gallimard, France's largest press, which enables him to publish young talents.

Torn between a deep religious faith and a sexuality that he perceives as abnormal, haunted by a poetic vocation he felt early on, the young Sénac, barely an adult at the beginning of this correspondence, tries to find a path in the social and Cultural universe of the Colony. Initiated into literature via Algerianism, which already belongs to Algeria's past, he reveres and admires his elder like most fellow men of his generation. Since the beginning he was a critic of Camus's works; soon he will be at his side in the tough battle of *The Rebel*.

The first exchange between these two men brings us to the period immediately after World War II: afflicted with an illness that Camus knew well, Jean Sénac had to stay at the Rivet Sanatorium near Algiers and was bored there. In his first letter, on June 16, 1947, he expresses his fervor for texts like *Nuptials*, and the pride that he feels as an Algerian for the success of his elder. Camus answers very quickly, very affectionately, as though to "a friend," to "a younger brother."

A sustained correspondence followed—the same one that interests us here—as well as several meetings in Algeria and in France. The first of these occurred the following winter, during the Sidi Madani meetings,[1] where Sénac, whose artistic models were still terribly conventional, became acquainted with Jean Cayrol, Francis Ponge, Louis Parrot, Brice Parain, and Jean Tortel—to whom he dedicated one of his first collections of poetry, *Sept poèmes de là-bas.*[2] A photograph shows them there, side by side, Camus gazing attentively and indulgently upon his young friend, who was smiling timidly: "I have the greatest trust in you. You have an innocence (like Schiller spoke of the admirable Greek innocence) that is irreplaceable."

And he, the renowned writer, proved this immediately by multiplying his efforts to publish the young, unknown poet in the capital's literary journals, by investing himself personally in the two reviews—*Soleil* and *Terrasses*—created by Sénac, by helping him financially during his stay in France from September 1950 to September 1952, and finally by bringing into his collection, under the simple title *Poèmes*, the first poems of a young friend who had experienced so many hardships.[3] After a few encounters, the "My dear Sénac" from the first exchanges evolved into an affectionate "Mi hijo," and until 1954, with the tragic events that will separate them, the young poet knows that he can count on "the firm and real friendship" (*Carnets*, 1954) of his elder.

Around these two friends there's a whole network of "brothers of the sun" who are anxiously anticipating the coming years: In Algiers, the painter Galliéro, who was already close to both of them; Emmanuel Roblès who, during the Sidi Madani meetings, published *Forge* in order to weave "tonic friendships" that could transgress all the divisions that were emerging; Jules Roy, who as an officer was close to the colonial camp; and a little later Jean Pélégri and Jean-Pierre Millecam, whose novels were published by Camus with Gallimard.

In France, mostly with the help of his illustrious friend, Sénac became acquainted with René Char, "a poet irrigated with vital blood" with his review *Empédocle*, where he published two poems by Sénac; also with Jean Daniel and the short-lived press Vineta that almost published his first collection; and finally with Paul Eluard and François Mauriac.

On the Algerian side, Sénac was already close to Baya, Kateb Yacine, Mohamed Dib, Jean Amrouche . . . artists who, like him, had chosen their allegiance. But he hid for a long time the connections he was establishing with the nationalist circles, leading some to believe that it was Camus who warned him of the upcoming revolution, when in fact it was Sénac who announced it to the author of *The Rebel*—one of the important contributions of Hamid Nacer-Khodja's essay.

. . .

It's a story of men confronted by history, since in the early 1950s, in North Africa as in other parts, decolonization was on the march. In Algeria, the uprisings of Sétif and Guelma, on May 8, 1945, and the repression that followed made a lasting impact. In the following years, serious disruptions foreshadowed a global rebellion that would spread to Morocco, Indochina, Madagascar . . . Sénac knew it; he comments or mentions them in his writings, increasingly politicized.

One cannot help but think that his friendship with Camus was evolving under a great misunderstanding. Introduced by René Char, Sénac's *Poèmes*, which were nonpolitical, didn't get published by Gallimard until the end of June 1954, a few months before the "bloody All Saints' Day."[4] But by that time his ideas and his unpublished work had already evolved considerably, "from an aesthetic Algeria . . . to a true journal of operations for a nascent Algerian nation," according to Hamid Nacer-Khodja. As for Camus, he presented *The Just* in 1949 and published *The Rebel* in 1951, creating a controversy during which Sénac came to his defense.

But the young poet is now concerned with the issue of political *engagement*. Prophesying that "Soon the steel will refuse the neck," he wonders what form this engagement will take: with the pen or with action? Camus, paternal as usual, gives him advice: concerning *Terrasses*, with which he became involved, Camus warns Sénac of the danger of "political colonization, whether direct or indirect, of the Right or of the Left" (letter of October 31, 1952). As for the resistance, "it's easier to dream of it than to return from it or even to see it coming" (undated postcard [August 29, 1953]).

. . .

It's a tragic story. When the armed conflict begins, an overwhelming responsibility lands on the shoulders of Albert Camus. In the minds of those who were close to him, and in the eyes of international opinion, he represented from then on the "intellectual conscience," a sort of "Master of Absolute," whom Sénac opposes in his poem from September 1956 as the committed poet he wants to be. Camus's philosophy, his work, his journalistic articles, his endeavors, everything gave the impression that he would make judicious and firm choices, that his attitude would meet the expectations of the small cenacle that had formed around him.

Like all of his friends, Jean Sénac continues to place a lot of hope in the actions and words of the great writer: he's aware of his troubles with the metropolitan Left, notices his interventions, follows his trips—he's worried for him and says so: to the Memmi brothers, with whom he was corresponding, he announces that "Camus is going to address the North African tragedy in terms that will alienate the entire Left." On March 28, 1955, following an interview at Gallimard, Sénac had imagined with joy that his Master "[would] accept to join publicly, and in a precise manner, the Algerian struggle by showing his solidarity with Ferhat Abbas."

Nevertheless, when a few months later Jules Roy begs Camus to take a stance against the repression, his letter remains unanswered and it's finally he who has to do so in *L'Express*. Sick, tired, and concerned with his wife's serious health issues, and very affected by the failure of his call for a civil truce (Algiers, January 22, 1956), Camus won't go any further than his declarations of intent.

The famous Stockholm episode in December 1957—which Sénac summarized as follows: "Camus was my father. Having to choose between my father and Justice, I have chosen Justice"—ends their friendship. And the definitive breakup between the Master, who bemoans "his lost country," and the student, who's enthralled at the idea of a budding nation, occurs during a final meeting, stormy and tragic, at Gallimard late in the winter of 1958. Bitter ending for Camus, who called his protégé a "Scipion" and a "little cutthroat"; and infinitely painful for Sénac, wounded in his admiration and his affection:

> The Poet of the Absolute
> Near the Jabbok ford laughed in the Friend's face
> He kept his hands pure (like icebergs!)
> while the poet wrote frenetically.
> And the Poet loved him.

After the passing away of Rabah Belamri (1946–1995), Hamid Nacer-Khodja (1953–2016) took on the heavy and exhilarating task of perpetuating the memory of Jean Sénac, who was brutally disappeared forty-five years ago. With this essay, he reveals an essential chapter of Sénac's biography, later completed by Bernard Mazo.

But he does even more, giving us a page in Franco-Algerian history, the Algerian War, and the tragedy of the *pied-noir* community. A painful page, a difficult page to turn—many recent events, political positions on Camus, more than fifty years after his death and the Independence of Algeria, are there to prove it—whose complexity we can now better understand through the intelligent and measured tone of this book.

Preface by the Translator

Part I

I began the translation of Hamid Nacer-Khodja's book in 2015, after the publication of Sénac's correspondence with Algerian writer Mohammed Dib, along with a manifesto that the poet wrote in 1957, *The Sun under the Weapons*, and notes from a conference of young poets in Constantine, in 1972.[1] I had visited Nacer-Khodja before that, in 2010 and 2014, as I was doing research for my dissertation on Sénac's revolutionary poetry. As a matter of fact, *Albert Camus, Jean Sénac, or the Rebel Son* was the book that first sparked my interest in the poet and that led me to Nacer-Khodja's home in Djelfa. He was a most attentive host and generous scholar, giving me access to his personal documents, even photocopying the material that I needed at the local photocopy shop.

The process of translating the essay and the correspondence started amid Nacer-Khodja's fight with cancer, which ultimately claimed his life in September 2016. The trace of this friendship is present in this book, which is both a revival and a reminiscence. My intention was to remain as close to Hamid's language as possible, in order for the reader to sense the density and precision with which he analyzes a correspondence that has personal significance to him. There is something filial in Hamid's writing, a concern for the father-son relation that perhaps speaks to a deeper, perhaps more personal, search within himself. Is there not always a certain element of autobiography when writing of the other, which Hamid identifies in Sénac's own writing and poetry?

Part II

Hamid Nacer-Khodja, poet, essayist, and journalist, was director of Literature and Languages at the University of Djelfa, and dedicated much of his life to the work of Jean Sénac, whom he met as a young poet in 1969. At the time, Sénac was running his widely popular program on Radio Alger, featuring young Algerian poets along with prominent Third World and North American poets.[2] Aside from his radio show, which was shut down in 1972, Sénac was organizing readings all over Algeria and received young poets at the tiny basement apartment he occupied in the center of Algiers. Although he had been a strong supporter of the Algerian Revolution from the beginning, Sénac became increasingly marginalized starting in 1967, for his European background, his increasingly critical stance towards the Algerian military government, and for his open homosexuality (which he graphically expressed in his later erotic poetry).

Many years after Sénac's assassination in 1973, for reasons that are still unclear, and his eventual disappearance from Algeria's cultural memory, Hamid Nacer-Khodja began his long endeavor to recover the poet. Dedicating his master's thesis on Jean Sénac and Albert Camus at Paris IV Sorbonne (1995), Nacer-Khodja continued his doctoral research on Jean Sénac's critical work at the University of Montpellier III, under the direction of Guy Dugas (2005). Aside from this extensive archival research, published in 2013 under the title *Jean Sénac, critique algérien*, Nacer-Khodja published numerous essays on the poet, bringing to light Sénac's essential role as poet, critic (both artistic and literary), and editor during a crucial time of transition in Algeria's quest for identity, and later independence. Among these works is the present volume, originally published in 2004 by Paris-Méditerranée, now out of print.

Nacer-Khodja provides here a vivid and essential testimony of two men who, in their friendship, expressed both their intimate appreciation for each other and the passion they held for a literature that spoke to the immediate concerns of their times. Interwoven, and at times indistinguishable, is the love between the men and that of a literature caught in the torments of the Algerian War. In that sense, these letters, especially those written after 1954, are not a theory on the anticolonial struggle; they are that struggle incarnated, lived, and fought as a relational conflict—a conflict of lovers (in the purest sense), especially of a young and passionate poet with regard to an elder and affectionate mentor.

This role of mentorship becomes all the more powerful and conflictual when it coincides with political upheaval and the traumatic rupture between Algeria and France, which becomes mirrored in the ultimate breach in the friendship between Sénac and Camus in 1958, at the height of the Algerian War. One could almost read Sénac and Camus as allegories of the brutal colonial severance between an aspiring young nation and its colonizer. It is also the confrontation between a revolutionary poet who sides with the Algerian cause, and understands its violence, and the public intellectual, recipient of the Nobel Prize, who defends a certain dominant order.

The profound testimony of Sénac and Camus's correspondence speaks to the crucial role of literary friendships in revealing the politics at stake. Sénac was an avid proponent of this dialogue in his three literary reviews—*M*, *Soleil*, and *Terrasses*—which Camus supported as contributor and advisor. Camus himself had published Sénac's poetry in his collection *Espoir*, along with the writings of René Char and Simone Weil. Yet, in both these endeavors one finds different attitudes toward the political in literature. While Sénac saw a need for ethnic representation among the authors that he featured in his reviews, Camus envisioned a more neutral literary stance, one that seemed to privilege a more European orientation, instead of a multicultural approach representing the many voices of Algeria in the context of colonialism. This difference was already an indication of the ideological differences between the two men, in terms of literature's direct reference to a political cause. To Sénac's explicit commentary, which became increasingly radical as the Algerian War progressed, Camus preferred the more abstract and indirect allusions, such as those he voiced in *The Rebel* and *The Just*.

While the recent publication of the *Algerian Chronicles* in English has somewhat displaced the common view of an existentialist and romantic Camus, bringing to light his torment during the Algerian War and his existential dilemma in the face of public opinion (his support of a French Algeria and his condemnation of French colonial practices, including torture and terrorism), his correspondence with Sénac further reveals an ambivalence that borders on lucidity. One sees firsthand the slow and tragic deterioration of a friendship, Sénac's desperate attempts to bring Camus over to the Algerian cause, and finally the bitter breakup between the poet who continues to venerate his mentor and the Nobel recipient who retreats into silence after accusing his young protégé of "glorifying the bomb that indiscriminately kills the child and the dreadful 'blinded' adult."

Sénac's response to Camus in 1957 had all the marks of Fanon's *Wretched of the Earth*, published four years later in 1961. Far from an apology of violence, or even a support thereof, Sénac understands the despair of the Algerian people and its slow transformation into hatred:

> The dreadful climate of exasperation that the Algerians were plunged into after one hundred years of rejected friendship, of exploited patience, of betrayed hope, has pushed them to their limits I believe—including the political leaders (who under these circumstances are reacting like the rest of the people, with terrible honesty, a furious and honest innocence)—and to respond to the endless lies and calculated crimes with a kind of rage, a deadly embrace.

One finds a striking similarity between Sénac's depiction of the colonized in his letter to Camus, and the following passage from Fanon's groundbreaking analysis:

> But let us return to this atmospheric violence, this violence rippling under the skin. We have seen it as it develops how a number of driving mechanisms pick it up and convey it to an outlet. In spite of the metamorphosis imposed on it by the colonial regime in tribal or regional conflicts, violence continues to progress, the colonized subject identifies his enemy, puts a name to all of his misfortunes, and casts all his exacerbated hatred and rage in this new direction.[3]

Sénac was well aware of Fanon's writings prior to *The Wretched of the Earth* in the many articles the latter edited and published for the FLN clandestine newspaper *El Moudjahid*, upon his exile in Tunisia sometime in 1957.[4] Sénac was in close contact with the French Federation of the FLN, and collaborated with the printing of *El Moudjahid* on the presses of Subervie, publisher of Sénac's manifesto *The Sun under the Weapons*, published in October 1957[5] (which precipitated his falling out with Camus). In what direction ideas were flowing at the time is impossible to say, but what is certain is that Sénac gave emotional substance to the struggle expressed by Fanon and many others, which he again used in his condemnation of Camus, even though both were experiencing the Algerian War from afar, as did many exiled Algerian revolutionaries.

The conflict between Sénac and Camus on Algeria had much to do with the real divisions between proponents of an independent Algeria and those who believed that Algeria should remain French. The letters, however, reveal a deeper misunderstanding with the problem of extremism and the difficulty of a dialogue amidst the passion of war that both the poet and the writer came to represent. In reality both Camus and Sénac envisioned a nation where all communities could cohabit and transcend the legacies of colonialism and oppression. According to Guy Dugas, "the first believed that Algerians would recognize on their own that independence wouldn't benefit them, the second that this independence would bring about the great reconciliation of communities and citizens." Both were mistaken in their vision and blinded in the passion of their disagreement, which at times resembles that of a love affair.

The father-son dynamic that Hamid Nacer-Khodja privileges in his essay could be superimposed on that of disciple and master, and ultimately lead to intimate love between men. It is only through a "deep" love, whatever the ilk, that one can understand the deep disappointments that each had in the other. The disappointment of this failed relationship transposes itself into the internecine conflict between France and Algeria. In other words, this friendship is what was at stake in the context of the Algerian War.

Part III

The importance of Nacer-Khodja's work also lies in the Algerian perspective it brings to an otherwise forgotten correspondence. While the scholarship on Camus is abundant, Sénac still struggles for recognition on both sides of the Mediterranean. Bringing this correspondence to light is therefore more than archival. It's a resistance to historical oblivion and to certain facile readings of Camus and the Algerian conflict. Nacer-Khodja's lifelong dedication to Jean Sénac's work is crucially significant, in Algeria, in France, and beyond, speaking for a marginalized gay *pied-noir* poet who took on the Algerian cause against one of its most prominent voices, and who could speak for hidden aspirations of young poets such as Nacer-Khodja himself. This cause lives on today among Algerian writers and poets who look toward Sénac as the bridge between communities that have been torn apart by history.

Nacer-Khodja's detailed account, which unfolds in minute increments, speaks in the present moment of his own questioning. He isn't writing in the past of the correspondence, but in the present effort to decipher and understand the nature of a friendship that held so much hope and potential. Perhaps Nacer-Khodja is also writing as the young poet searching for his own lost mentor, and the lost hopes of Algerian independence that Sénac encapsulates in so many ways. For there is a loss here, a missing link in Algeria's transition to independence, which is arguably Nacer-Khodja's underlying concern. In the face of Camus's deafening silence, which in many ways has engulfed much of the Algerian narrative, there is Sénac's cry for recognition, for the hopes and the aspirations of the Algerian people in the face of official discourse (both France's and later that of the post-independence military establishment).

Nacer-Khodja also reveals to us Sénac's passionate reading and understanding of Camus's work, which comes across in the early radio shows that the poet directed on Radio Alger. His introduction of Camus in his 1949 show "A poet of the joie de vivre: Albert Camus" is an extraordinary rendition of a writer commonly presented as "philosopher of the absurd." Sénac was constantly redeeming Camus from the simplistic interpretations that became so common in France and later in the United States, especially after the publication of *The*

Stranger in 1946. It is worth revisiting the novel based on Sénac's vision that there is lyrical poetry in Meursault, and that Camus "sometimes sings, sometimes wakes up like his Stranger, 'stars upon his face,' feeling 'the wonderful peace of the sleeping summer flow into him like a tide.'" Sénac's early readings of Camus are all the more moving given the tragic and desperate tone of their last exchanges.

The element of correspondence and mentorship, not to mention friendship, is finally an essential contribution of this book, one that continues to provide insight into the process behind the work of writers. One finds the continuing role of mentorship between Sénac and Nacer-Khodja, between Nacer-Khodja and Dugas (both first met each other in the late '70s), and within my own research on Sénac. Dugas provided a new preface to this translation, in honor of his former student, and generously clarified a few questions I had when translating Nacer-Khodja's essay. As much as this is a work about writers, it is one that highlights the role of affection and love between "men of letters"—men who expressed a deep commitment in their friendships and in their work.

In the tradition of "exchange," the translation of *Albert Camus, Jean Sénac, or the Rebel Son* from the French into the English, was informed by my bilingual background, and the work with my friend and coconspirator Kate Tarlow Morgan, writer, dancer, and editor. The technical labor of honing the words of scholar, poet, novelist, and revolutionary was enriched by a comradeship that had already been established in previous collaborations. Kate's dance/performance "A Letter from a Friend," based on the early texts of French poet Paul Valéry and interwoven with my own personal journal entries as a young man, galvanized our creative relationship and invited the intimacy of this present project of close reading and translation. Alongside such detailed textual reading, was our assiduous co-correcting and sharpening of the "message," as is the responsibility of translators and their faithfulness to the original thought and language.

During one of our conversations, Kate wondered what might have happened had Camus not disappeared in a car accident in 1960, had the exchange with Sénac mended after the unavoidable outcome of the Algerian War, had Sénac himself survived the assassination attempt in 1973. This question was perhaps very much at the back of Nacer-Khodja's mind, reflected in his own sense of loss and his extraordinary effort to reveal this moving correspondence.

The dialogue between Sénac and Camus was a profound reflection of their time, of the hopes and aspirations of the colonized, of France's failure to understand the oppression of the Algerian people. This correspondence might have had a different destiny—just as the Algerian War might have had a different outcome had both sides (or multiple sides) found common ground concerning the future of the Algerian nation—and had Camus and Sénac escaped their tragic fate.

Introduction

L iterature and politics have maintained a rich relationship in French literature—which can't be covered here—to the extent that the real aesthetic autonomy of the former didn't keep it from influencing the discourse of the latter. Literature produced in colonial Algeria, particularly by native writers, has gone far beyond its borders. Artistic creation (the embodiment of a fiction or of a lived experience) was not able to exclude a substratum of being and modes of behavior that were fundamentally problematic. The friendship between Jean Sénac and Albert Camus constitutes a "referential field" for a literature that confronted politics during the overwhelming rise of Algerian nationalism.

The meeting between Jean Sénac and Albert Camus, mentioned briefly in Sénac's biography, and even more briefly in Camus's, remains poorly understood.[1] Those who wrote on the subject aggravated this lack of understanding since, due to missing information, they multiplied errors and inaccuracies.[2]

Also, in the perspective of a literary history that imposes its own methods of investigation, this study is intended as an informative presentation of a relationship that lasted for over a decade (1947–1958). It is built mainly on the basis of writings published by the two writers, but it also relies on many unpublished documents: correspondence between the two men, their common friends René Char and Jean Grenier, their publisher Gallimard, as well as manuscripts, personal notebooks, and radio programs of Sénac.[3] Given the exceptional nature of this personal and literary friendship and, at the same time, the incomplete nature of these essential documents, we must not rely exclusively on the evidence of the texts. The poet, who spoke almost exclusively of himself,[4] including through the "other"—while fabulating and fabricating his own persona—has put his life into his writings and his writings into his life.[5] As for the writer, it was—in principle—a miracle not having to speak of one's self,[6] since the life of a man is more interesting than his works.[7]

We therefore had to resort to other, external proofs consisting of testimonials from reliable sources: Jean de Maisonseul,[8] close friend of Sénac and of Camus, and Jacques Miel, Sénac's adopted son and executor of his will. Even if they are only modest additions to our knowledge of the two authors—especially for Camus—the body of documents and information gathered here is nevertheless noteworthy in that it allows us to appreciate the quality (and the tribulations!) of their friendship. It also brings us additional details on their opinions and/or literary creations.

Within this framework, this study follows the parallel paths of their lives and especially Sénac's relation to Camus's texts, particularly those that relate to a political discourse. Politics and literature have been, in this regard, in a constant interaction within the works and the lives of these two men. Each of them, in their own way and to varying degrees, supported the idea of a committed literature while simultaneously being participants in and witnesses to their times. In confronting the positions of these two authors through a variety of texts and testimonies in which the stated, not stated, almost stated, or suggested collide—we will reflect upon the writer's sincerity, exposing for example the gaps and/or connections that exist between the attitudes and the writings of both men.

The Algerian War, begun on November 1st, 1954, was the historical event that disrupted this friendship—first literary, then turning quickly into a story of men—and led it toward a difficult, but inevitable breakup. Thus, the different stages of the friendship between Sénac and Camus can be divided into two larger periods:

- A literary filiation that developed into the relation of a son with his father, becoming increasingly difficult because of the expectations they had of each other (1947–1954).
- The rebellion, then the breakup of the "son" with a "father" who became the "enemy" because of the revolutionary war (1954–1958), and to whom he would remain faithful *post mortem* (1960–1973).

PART I

From a Literary Father to an Impossible Father (1947–1954)

CHAPTER 1

Birth of a Friendship

n 1946, Jean Sénac—barely twenty years old and a virtually unknown burgeoning poet—publicly acknowledged his indebtedness, if not his affiliation, to Camus, the author of *Noces* [*Nuptials*].[1] This "little essential book" was one of Sénac's most important discoveries, appearing in lyrical echoes and sensual resonances throughout his own work.[2] His gratitude was expressed through poems[3] he dedicated to the writer whose texts he had reviewed many times over the years.[4] As a literary critic,[5] Sénac displayed a great knowledge of Camus's work, which exemplified for him "dignity, French literature and Algerian concern for mankind."[6]

His admiration for the other local writers, whether European or Arabo-Berber—most of whom grew out of a declining Algerianism as well as the fast-growing École d'Alger—was just as strong given that "our profoundly human culture has solidified and continues to solidify Algerian and French fraternity."[7] Furthermore, Sénac was in contact with most of the writers who had represented the two literary schools of colonial Algeria, in a post–World War II Algiers that had kept an aura of "the capital of French literature in exile."[8] This "Algiers" is where Sénac had settled after his release from the air force (where he had been conscripted as a volunteer from October 31, 1944, to March 6, 1946). Whether part of the Association of Algerian Writers, assembled around Jean Pomier and his review *Afrique* (for example, Edmond Brua, his first teacher), or gathered around publisher Edmond Charlot and his bookstore Les Vraies Richesses (with Emmanuel Roblès, Jules Roy, Gabriel Audisio, etc.), these writers—all of them admiring friends of Camus—were either close friends of Sénac, encouraging him in the art of writing, or those he frequented in the literary and artistic circle founded in June 1946, "Le Cercle Lélian."[9]

It was upon the insistence of artist and painter Sauveur Galliéro,[10] a mutual friend he saw frequently starting in 1946, that Sénac decided to contact Camus. It was nevertheless Claude de Fréminville, thankful for Sénac's long article on his novel *Buñoz*,[11] who recommended[12] that he contact directly the famous publisher and writer in Paris.[13] In a letter he writes to Camus on June 16, 1947—while hospitalized at the Rivet Sanatorium* (today called Meftah) for a serofibrinous pleurisy on the left lung—Sénac fully reveals his personality: that of a man who draws a subtle self-portrait in his writing, speaking almost exclusively of himself, even when it's concerning the other.

In his letter to Camus, Sénac fulfills a long-repressed desire, and expresses among other things his admiration for the writer's work and for the poems of Blanche Balain.[14] "I love and I speak of those that I love, of what I love," he writes, thereby giving the guiding principle of his critical aesthetic: to speak only of works by Algerian writers, many of whom will become his friends—in short, to write about the words of his own people. Psychology as the foundation for critical freedom is nothing new. For Sénac, this practice became a paradigm that he could temper but not control, especially concerning Camus when he attempts to separate the man from his writings.†

---

* With the help of Mr. and Mrs. Brua.

† According to Guy Dugas, Sénac's critique was—far from all theory—one of proximity, of friendship, which he tried to balance (to temper according to Hamid Nacer-Khodja) with more objectivity. That was especially true, in his relation to Camus, after the publication of *The Just* and of *The Rebel*. These works were symptomatic of what would later separate the two men, i.e., the use of terrorist violence, which Sénac accepted and which Camus absolutely refused. Sénac at that time believed that he could separate in Camus the man of literature

In this letter, Sénac also sends to his famous recipient a photograph of the "little poet from Oran, today in a sanatorium," reading *Noces* in bed ("Ah Camus, thank you for that little book"), as well as poems that display a constant search for technique in the form, which he hopes, even "demands," will receive the severe critique he expected from the majority of his other correspondents (writers, review editors, publishers, etc.). He hopes that his own texts will provide Camus with a "little sun and fervor from Africa, from our home," since "we are proud in Algeria . . . of [the writer's] added fame" following the recent Prix des Critiques award for his novel *The Plague*.

Sénac received a response from Camus on June 24, 1947, which he describes in his personal diary as "a beautiful and affectionate letter that warms my heart."[5] He goes as far as replicating its first sentence in a letter he sends to Blanche Balain.[6] That first "Camusian"[7] correspondence is in many ways a strong testimony since it already reveals the nature of a friendship that was immediately born between the two men. Camus, as usual, responded on NRF [*Nouvelle Revue Française*] letterhead. His letter was nevertheless mailed from Panelier (Haute-Loire), where he was resting with his family after the publication of *The Plague* in early June 1947.[8] "Few letters have touched me as much as yours," he writes, as though to a "younger brother" with whom he shares three crucial traits; whereas in his letter Sénac ironically had questioned: "Affinities between him and me? Impossible!"

The first common trait was a community of the land: "What comes from there is always dear to me"; Camus, who had always been generous in heart and mind with the men of Algeria, seen as human beings no matter where they came from, adds "we are all brothers over there."

Second, the two men were tacitly complicit in their disease, which Camus had acknowledged ("It's an illness that benefits Algerians. In ten years it has allowed me to produce the work of two men"). Underlying this statement, as a corollary, is the recurrent idea of death and suicide, the "only serious philosophical problem" according to Camus in his preliminary critical essay *The Myth of Sisyphus*;[9] "a wrenchingly avid contest" Sénac writes in his masterpiece,

---

with whom he fundamentally disagreed, and the man of action whom he still supported (like many others in Algeria).

Avant-Corps [Forebody].[20] Death would always be present in their works[21] and in their lives, which for both began in November and ended prematurely at the age of forty-six, a coincidence that will confound both their friends and enemies. Strange destinies, unrelated at first, of a tandem that rested nevertheless on so many common traits: the same happy childhood spent in poverty under the sun and in working-class neighborhoods (Belcourt in Algiers and Saint Eugène in Oran); mothers with similar backgrounds, both originally Catalan of Spanish blood, both having worked as cleaning ladies, but also so different in temperament (silent in the case of Camus, who never benefited from her influence; a fervent and garrulous Catholic in the case of Sénac, who inherited both traits). Finally, an absent father leading to a historical and a personal quest, in vain for the orphan born under the star of death (Camus was barely a year old when he lost his father, who died from his wounds during the Battle of the Marne, on October 11, 1914), and for the natural son born under the star of anonymity (Sénac never knew his father).

The last subject, where the two men converge, was paradoxically religion. "Christian anarchist doesn't bother me,"[22] says Camus as an agnostic who subtly differentiates himself from atheism.[23] As for Sénac, his initial faith, a crucible for his poetry and for his struggles, would evolve over the years towards a form of Christianity without the Church, or even skillfully sacrilegious agnosticism (a "god without the formula").[24]

Even though "he wasn't keen on poetry,"[25] Camus immediately became interested in Sénac's verse and remains one of its most illustrious critics. After reviewing several of his texts, he adds: "Your poems are not bad" and "you have talent, for sure."

Lastly, Camus shares more personal information concerning his work, which he views—as usual—as work in progress ("I have barely begun to know my language"), or his private life (his plans to visit his mother in the fall). Autographing on a separate sheet of paper, he promises Sénac to have his publisher send him a copy of *The Plague*. Promise kept, since the poet mentions it in an article published on July 8, 1947: "Albert Camus: A great writer born in Oran."[26]

The article is notable for its literary chauvinism, sometimes deliberately regional and fabricated (Camus wasn't born in Rivoli, a precinct of Oran[27]), sometimes exact and legitimate ("Camus has just devoted his first novel to his native land"). This was a perceptive insight on *The Plague*, for Camus saw *Noces* as an essay and *The Stranger* as a narration.

The article reveals, most importantly, that "Camus's beautiful work, *The Myth of Sisyphus*, would soon be followed by an essay on *The Rebel.*" One wonders how, in the summer of 1947, Sénac knew of an essay that was still a project[28] in the lengthy formal process common to all of Camus's works. The answer would further reveal Sénac's familiarity with the writer's work, through mutual friends mentioned earlier and the many articles he read on the author.[29]

Soon after, on September 30, 1947, Sénac contributes another article[30] on Camus. He immediately corrects his mistake concerning the author's birthplace, after receiving some information from Emmanuel Roblès,[31] which he repeats almost textually. Following an overview of Camus's major literary and philosophical works, with large extracts, Sénac insists on the "Algerianism" of Camus. Despite the latter's universality, in the "surgical precision . . . of a modern sensibility" faced with chaos and the Absurd, Sénac nevertheless believes that Camus remains the "North African literary leader," as "all of his books reveal the latent presence of an Algerian temperament, and the image of man fashioned by our sky, our land, dispenser of riches without giving lessons."

Sénac sees in this writing a literary regionalism even though it acquires a global audience thanks to Camus. The latter will nevertheless express some reservations concerning this vision of literature, as did the other members of the École d'Alger. Finally, in his article, Sénac mentions a forthcoming movie adaptation of *The Plague* with Jean Gabin as leading actor. This factual piece of information, while premature, is surprising since Camus first mentioned it on November 15, 1947,[32] and refuted it on November 28 in an interview with Emmanuel Roblès at Radio Algeria.[33]

●　　■　　■

This first epistolary exchange (referred to above) was the beginning of a sustained correspondence between the two men, even though it wasn't regular. Camus, who was still on vacation in Panelier, "was glad to receive" another letter from Sénac, which he responded to on July 13, 1947. His wholehearted reply contains vital information on his projects. Again he addresses the poet's struggle with illness: "I will be very pleased once I know that you are fully recovered and out of your little cloister." He also asks him if he needs "anything," having read "in the newspapers that people over there were malnourished and that there were incidents."[34] That last point proves how much Camus was informed on In his response, Camus mentions his personal life (vacations, children) and speaks of three ongoing projects, two of which were significant:

1. An aesthetic theater, involving "the spoken and mimed transposition of the play *Journal of the Plague Year* by Daniel Defoe," which he dedicated to Jean-Louis Barrault. This play would become, as we know, the "total theater" of *The State of Siege* after the original idea was abandoned.
2. A trip to South America planned for spring 1948. After much deliberation, Camus ended up traveling to Brazil and Argentina only, in June and August 1949.[35]
3. Again his plan to travel to Algeria in the fall in order to see his mother "who is old now." Camus did visit Algiers in October 1947, and was hoping to meet Sénac, but they apparently never saw each other given that the poet was still hospitalized at Rivet. Such an encounter would certainly have been mentioned in his journals, especially his *Journal du sana* [Sanatorium journal].[36]

In this letter, Camus goes from "Sending you my fraternal thoughts" in his previous letter to "thinking of you, very affectionately." The lexical shift indicates a favorable evolution in Camus's feelings for someone who's become more than a simple correspondent: Sénac has gained a sympathy that will quickly turn into friendship.

■   ■   ■

The first long-awaited meeting between the two happened on or close to March 2, 1948, during the Sidi Madani Cultural Meetings [Rencontres culturelles de Sidi Madani] (near Blida) organized by the Algerian Service for the Youth Movement and Popular Education, held at "La Citadelle" Cultural Center.

Several references confirm this. First, a study by Jean Déjeux[37] suggesting that Camus and Sénac met in Sidi Madani sometime during their respective stays: Camus from March 2 to 13, and Sénac from February 26 to March 4. What was only a hypothesis for the distinguished bibliographer and essayist on literature of the Maghreb in French [*littérature maghrébine d'expression française*] becomes a fact in an article published by Sénac in his own mimeographed review *M*[38] and in his unfinished letter to Jean Daniel.[39] In these documents the poet mentions his meeting with Camus, as well as the latter's participation in a discussion at Sidi Madani.

Finally, a third letter that Camus wrote to Sénac on April 7, 1948, upon his return to France, stating that he "was happy to have met him. Less so to be back in Paris, its labyrinth and its shabby Minotaur," habitual expressions from the author that take on here a significant tone. In this letter Camus again expresses his appreciation for Sénac's poetry: "You have the freshest and the most authentic talents." He valued *Mesure d'homme*,[40] a collection yet to be published, and added this notable appraisal: "I have the greatest trust in you. There is in you a certain *naiveté* (like Schiller who spoke of the remarkable Greek *naiveté*)."

Camus ends his letter with "Faithfully," showing the appreciation that the two men now have for each other. The poet is overjoyed: the master indeed repeats the expression from *Nuptials*, "Greek insolence and innocence,"[41] to describe Sénac's poetry and way of life, an affirmation of the body's freedom despite a Christianity that "strives to suspend desire."[42]

Sénac—still recovering at the Rivet Sanatorium, where he worked as the director's clerk and bursar—receives a fourth letter from Camus, sent from Paris on September 7, 1948. It's a response to Sénac's critical essay on Isidore Isou, the theorist of *letterisme*, who had "amused"[43] him: "you are worth all the Isous in the world." Camus further clarifies his opinion of the writer: "All the provocations in the world can't give Isou any fame, or great talent. He will serve only his publicity, which is not the same thing," since "that kind of work isn't worth a penny." It is worth recognizing the critic's accuracy concerning a writer whose fireworks, coinciding with the publication of *The Plague* (1947), were quickly forgotten. In the same letter Camus returns to Sénac's poetry: "You're making progress on a difficult road: the right one." He expresses a few thoughts, reflective of his best writing, on a life that "is hard in France. At home poverty is easy. Here is it cold and unforgiving. Sometimes it can kill."

■　■　■

After leaving the sanatorium on December 1, 1948, Jean Sénac returns to Algiers. He lives with his Albertin cousins in Bab-el-Oued, and in the Casbah with Sauveur Galliéro. Perhaps he met Camus again, who was in Algiers later that month visiting his aunt, Acault, after her operation.[44] This seems likely, since Sénac had a copy of Letters to a Young German with the autograph "to Jean Sénac, a little reminder of my formative years," dated 1948. Sénac would imitate theses letters many times in his own unpublished "Letters to a Friend," where he pities himself, unlike Camus who chastises.

Jean Sénac had started as sound director of a weekly literary show at Radio Algiers[45] on December 3, 1948. On October 26, 1949, he announces to Camus that he will produce a show titled "Nuptials with the world: A poet of the joie de vivre: Albert Camus."[46] Two main ideas are explored in these programs, which Sénac had already analyzed in his articles. The first one concerned Camus's philosophy, which celebrates pleasure in a country that "gives without holding back," while retaining a somewhat preoccupied lucidity. This intensity of life finds its expression in Camus's lyrical prose, even though he always denied being a poet. Referring to Camus's statement "I often have the (humiliating) impression that I understand nothing of poetry," Sénac suggests that "Algerians don't write poems; they are themselves a luminous summer poem." It's one of the poet's most recurrent premises: to live in reality is a triumph over literature. He concurs with the "Camusian" stance—so identifiable in his own poetry as well as in his literary and radiophonic writings—of the Algerian (European, or the French Algerian according to the terminology at the time) who remains speechless when confronted with the "invincible summer" and natural beauty. A second literary theme dear to Sénac is an "Algerianism" where Algeria is an eclectic ideal of continuous wants and desires. Camus is of course part of this "Algerianism."

In a letter to Camus, Sénac expresses his gratitude for the advice he was given and for the discovery of René Char ("It's thanks to you, since that evening in [Sidi] Madani when you mentioned it, that I discovered that poetry of man, which teaches me of rigor and honesty, truth and modesty"), and professes the following: "Four years ago I found my philosopher: Albert Camus. Around the same time came the fruitful revelation of the painter Sauveur Galliéro, my brother. Today, finally, I discover the poet that I was always searching for: René Char." This statement reveals a new "fundamental trinity," after the one of his adolescence (Victor Hugo, Paul Verlaine, and Edmond Brua), and anticipates a new trinity (Camus, Char, and Lorca).

From René Char, with whom he had been corresponding since October 25, 1949, Sénac receives his poetics (the sense of concise formulas and images, often with double or ambiguous meanings); from Galliéro, a pragmatism (the art of being man); and from Camus, a philosophy of life (that of a continuous and guiltless pleasure) despite a "modesty" that "sometimes breaks the skin to let the juice flow."[47] This modesty, an essential trait of the writer, was expressed in a legendary silence that the exuberant Sénac was unable to grasp.

In his response on November 7, 1949, Camus—who was in the middle of a tuberculosis relapse (reminding the poet, "It's an illness that you know well")—returns to Sénac's poetry. He was "so satisfied" with it that he found it necessary "to try to make your voice known." Camus, like Char, was a founding member on the editorial committee of *Empédocle*,[48] a Parisian literary review directed by Jean Vagne. Camus sends to Char a few texts by Sénac, which will be published[49] even though "the review publishes only a few poems"—even according to Char,[50] who made the final selection.[51] Finally, Camus's letter contains additional thoughts on Sénac's poetry, such as this other famous commentary: "You have a talent that doesn't owe anything to anyone—luminous and healthy—with real courage."

Yet, despite having written several collections, Sénac hadn't published any of them by late 1949. One of them, *Terre possible*, was being painstakingly developed (the project of his entire life!). This collection, to be published by Edmond Charlot in 1950, was going to be prefaced by Albert Camus,[52] according to a show on Radio Algiers on July 3, 1950—a hasty disclosure that could only have come from Sénac. Indeed, in a letter from December 16, 1949, Camus—still ill, in Paris—encourages Sénac to publish this collection, finding "that the selection seems good." When solicited for a preface ("text for publicity," he writes), Camus answers: "You can surely find a couple of lines in one of my letters," and adds: "If I could think and work, I would send you a more adequate text," for "your poems are beautiful, and I'm glad." Camus never did write the preface that Sénac, with permission, later wrote (in 1953) by combining two parts of a previously mentioned correspondence with Camus (that of April 7, 1948, and November 7, 1949), this with citations of Char's foreword to his first collection, *Poèmes*. This piece, which was often presented by Sénac and by publishers as Camus's "preface," was in reality only a "notice" that accompanied the volume. It is mentioned in Gallimard's bulletin.[53]

. . .

In this summer of 1950, Sénac was unable to edit his collection. Charlot was faced with financial difficulties that led to the closing of his Parisian press, but not his bookstore in Algiers, which remained open—after many moves—up until the eve of Algeria's independence, on July 3, 1962.[54] In response to this misfortune—despite the stubborn reluctance of his friend Sauveur Galliéro[55]—the poet applies for and obtains a visiting fellowship in literature (the other laureate being Galliéro for painting) from the Laurent-Vibert de Lourmarin Foundation, allocated by the general government of Algeria.[56] Sénac's old dream of going to France, in order to succeed intellectually and poetically, becomes reality. On August 1, 1950, he writes to Char, who hosts him at Isle-sur-la-Sorgue, and to Camus, who welcomes him to Paris. He writes to Camus, observing that "I really need that *choc*, that wonder and the hard trial no doubt of lost illusions." The latter informs Sénac, on August 12, 1950, that he would be away until September 1 (he was on vacation at Grand-Valtin in the Vosges) and that they would probably miss each other. He sends him several useful addresses, including most importantly his own, until the return of his secretary, "Suzanne Labiche" (who became Agnely through marriage). Suzanne Agnely would become an important mediator between the two men.

. . .

Jean Sénac was about to leave for France, for his first visit, a few days after the death of "Robert Randau the trailblazer"[57] (August 4, 1950), his second mentor with Brua. Acknowledging his debt towards him—yet repudiating him like so many others (one mentor chasing the other away during this period[58])—the poet writes in a notebook in January 1954:

The master is not the one we follow fearlessly or that we imitate. He is the one who teaches us, who invites us. The one who teaches us without complacency, selflessly, the craft, and the dignity of its practice.

Putting this to practice, the poet boards a ship to Marseille on September 3, 1950. Thus begins a new chapter in his life. His new mentors, Char, but mostly Camus, will have a fundamental role to play, providing him with kindness and affection. The friendship between these three writers will be tremendously productive for Sénac.

CHAPTER 2

Algerianism or *École d'Alger*

O n the eve of Camus's departure for France, a disagreement occurred between him and Sénac on the role of literature in Algeria. This was a precursor to future misunderstandings, despite the identical impressionist and "Tainian" revelations they experienced when reading André Gide (*The Fruits of the Earth*) and Jean Grenier (*Islands*). According to the poet,[1] they discussed their different points of view at the Sidi Madani meetings. Contrary to Camus, who voiced reservations on "regionalist" Algerian literature (regionalism was at the time upheld by the right-wing ideology of Barrès), Sénac defended "Barrèsism," or a literary provincialism—i.e., "indigenous" writing by French Algerian natives as well as by the new Muslim writers who expressed themselves in French, in Arabic, or in the Algerian dialect.

In this vein, Sénac published studies and articles in newspapers with extremist political leanings, from *Marches de France* (Attichy), a weekly magazine advocating for "international regionalism," or *L'Africain* (Algiers), another right-wing weekly magazine of the Republican Party for Freedom [Parti Républicain de la Liberté], to *Oran Républicain*, a daily newspaper published by the Popular Front [Front populaire] (writings published under the symbolic title *Visages d'Algérie* [Faces of Algeria]).² Sénac, still apolitical at the time, justified his eclectic contributions in an interview dated August 3, 1950: "I'm able to publish articles on Christian writers in a Communist newspaper, whereas the weekly magazine PRL [*Parti Républicain pour la Liberté*] included my ramblings on some other leftist poet or another . . . It was very funny!"³

Sénac's journalism developed ideas close to those of Algerianism, which is where he began. With the support of Edmond Brua and Robert Randau (since November 1945), Sénac joined the Association of Algerian Writers in April 1946 (after his release from the military).* He soon became assistant treasurer for the journal *Afrique*, Algerianism's "newsletter for critical reviews and ideas," and then later its assistant editor. In this bimonthly review he published twenty-two Parnassian poems instilled with Christian mysticism or mild social faith (he combined them later in the published collection *Mesure d'homme*, as noted above⁴), and a few brief literary and artistic chronicles.

Sénac retained two main ideas of Algerianism:

1. A predilection for inspiration that came exclusively from the deep Algeria and its people "equal in humanity" (Robert Randau),⁵ even though the condescending or sympathetic gaze was imbued with paternalism. This was contrary to the School of Algiers, which was generally interested only in the Mediterranean sensibility (sea, beaches, coastal cities). In a letter written on January 30, 1948, to the governor-general of Algeria—who had just given him a 10,000 francs grant as encouragement (with the support of Jean Pomier and Robert Randau)—the poet explains his role within the movement. He underlines that in his articles, particularly those in *Oran Républicain*, he strives to uncover, to observe, and to convey real life in Algeria, in all of its diversity, regardless of languages or origins.

2. The idea of an "Algerian native homeland" conveyed by Robert Randau, the only person that Sénac (who met him in Algiers in November 1945) addressed as "cher Maître" in his correspondence. Paradoxically, two characteristics—of great ideological importance regarding the "colonial

---

* Created in 1919–1920 and headed by Jean Pomier, this association sustained the literary movement [Algerianism].

(and not colonialist) writer," as Sénac would later add[6]—foreground the poet's pro-Algerian political activism:

a. On one hand, that an Algerian writer must know the Arab language, if not the country's Berber language. In his "novel" *Ébauche du père*, written in the middle of the Algerian War, Sénac reiterates Randau's position on the matter: "We form a nation with the Arab component, the Berber component. These are predominant. We must know their language."[7]

b. On the other hand, the need to live as a community with the Muslims and to include the Arabs and the Berbers in the formation of a new nation, that of "the Franco-Berber people," a people who want to be different from the French without severing their ties with France. Algerianism's claim of "aesthetic autonomy" must be adapted to a reversed politics of assimilation, no longer that of the indigenous with regard to the French, but of the French with the native population.

As for the *École d'Alger* (or "North African School of Literature," as Camus called it upon his return from New York in April 1946), Sénac was one of the first literary critics to argue against it by refuting some of its aspects. In an article curtly and explicitly titled "No, there isn't a North African school,"[8] he states that one cannot confine the writers born in North Africa and those from France or elsewhere who have settled there to a "restricted clan," "a circle with a doctrine and manifesto," or classify them "under a spectacular banner." It's merely a "bond of friendship," of "passionate and independent wills" with diverse aspirations and belonging to various communities (French, Spanish, Italian, Berber, Arab, Mediterranean) who want to bring "new and generous blood" to French literature. This contribution can be understood on two levels:

1. A Historical Level

There is, for Sénac, a continuity in North African literature that goes from Louis Bertrand (the only one that he does not favor) and Robert Randau to Camus, Roblès, Jean Amrouche, taking into account the Muslim writers who will form a "future indigenous school" (he mentions El Boudali Safir, Saâdeddine Bencheneb, and . . . Mohamed Laïd-Khalifa, Arab-speaking poet). This is a genuine plea for the "Algerian-French fraternity," an equilibrium between two parties that weren't yet irreconcilable for the poet. One should note that in his statement, Sénac includes all of the colonial literature (including those of travelers: Fromentin, Gide, etc.) that would later be called "colonial literature" after the Algerian independence.

2. A Thematic and Spatial Level

Sénac states that while all literary theories "have confronted and battled each other" in Algeria, the aforementioned writers "have always sung their love, their masculine beauty, their violence and their lust, on every note." With lyricism he mentions that the same blood pulsates in their hearts and in their works "with the marvelous rhythm of the sun and the sea." He considers that all these voices are physically committed to the same soil. Citing Camus,[9] Sénac concludes: "A land, a sky, a man fashioned by this land and this sky, this is history's last word." The distinctive geographical identity of these writers doesn't keep them from being part of French literature, given that their writing mimics—whether they want it or not, and despite their autonomist intentions—the particular traits of their counterparts in France.

Sénac avoids the debate pitting together the two literary movements that differ both in substance and content: Algerianism sees itself as an Algerian school, edited mainly in France for an audience that stays within its borders, contrary to the *École d'Alger*—first edited in Algiers, then soon after in Paris—which aspires and succeeds in becoming a school on both shores, turning itself toward the open sea and the outside world. As stated by Sénac in his first comprehensive study of French literature produced in Algeria,[10] both schools equally broaden "the influence of North Africa within French literature." Therefore he doesn't differentiate himself from either group, borrowing references from one (a deeply multilingual, multicommunitarian, and multiconfessional country) as well as from the other (sun, beaches, ocean). According to him, both are simply aesthetic schools with views and orientations that were more or less favorable to the Muslim population and writers, even if these were to remain under the influence of the "French City" (Randau). This ideology was obviously fundamentally colonialist, causing both Algerianism and the *École d'Alger* to be discarded at the start of the Algerian War, since its representatives—with the exception of Sénac, who evolved quickly —weren't ready to accept an independent Algeria.

It's nevertheless important to note that Sénac's literary concerns at that time (1947–1948) were not ideological or political. For example, in a review he wrote on the journal *Forge*, directed by Emmanuel Roblès and his friends in Algiers, he warns "against political temptations"[11] without further explanation. Far from the dominant political speech (oscillating between colonialism at its height and nationalism in various forms), Sénac solidified his humanist aspirations with the creation of the review *Soleil*[12] in 1949–1950, of which he was the founding member. Presenting itself as an intercommunitarian forum, the review welcomed unpublished texts by Mohamed Dib, Kateb Yacine, Mouloud Feraoun, and Ahmed Sefrioui. Nevertheless, the poet envisioned a timid political undertone, since he wanted to bear witness not only through writing, but through action. In an editorial project, he states that its "aim is to bring together young writers who want to express themselves on this African soil, to attest to a luminous and healthy spirit, to assert the fraternity and the hope of men despite their differences."[13] In January 1950, Sénac defines a similar objective in a letter to René Char: that the periodical should express "all of the fraternity and hope of men stamped upon this African soil so full of disagreements and wounds."[14] On the literary and human level, the poet calls for reconciliation, an attitude that would remain constant even during the Algerian War. As we will see, his support for one side didn't exclude understanding the other.

Nevertheless, in the early '50s, Sénac hadn't fully distanced himself from Algerianism and the *École d'Alger*. Despite his call for a cultural stance, the *Soleil* review didn't publish any ideological text (with the exception of the last volume, a special edition on Republican Spain). Yet on a personal level, after his right-wing tendencies that were partly due to the ideology of Algerianism, the poet's leftist leanings became increasingly noticeable. A distinctly humanist activism, born around 1949–1950, would quickly disintegrate and become political activism. In early summer of 1950, Sénac begins to frequent the nationalist circles of Algiers, "Communist friends, PPA or UDMA,"[15] as mentioned in a letter he wrote to Camus on August 1, 1950. In this letter he announces that he will be coming to France and returning to Algeria "in one or two years," as there are "still a few human values worth saving in the great chaos that's coming." The "racist and colonialist"[16] system is now relentlessly condemned, but only verbally or in private. The poet's first political pro-Algerian text would be written only three months later in Paris, in November 1950, in which he specifies that the Algerian artist "is not only the witness of freedom" but a "daily combatant" who should never "refuse the call for action."[17]

Sénac's wavering attitude, dominated by the emblematic figure of Camus, probably justified an article on the "greatness and decadence"[18] of this "professor of writing,"[19] who became a loved but difficult mentor (politically).

CHAPTER 3

The Son Faces the Father

hen Sénac arrived in Marseille, on September 4, 1950, Camus was still recovering from another bout of tuberculosis in Le Grand-Valtin (Vosges), after a stay in Cabris (Alpes-Maritimes) with his family. Although he was in the region for tourism, Sénac didn't meet him and went directly to the castle of Lourmarin.

After a brief stay in Lourmarin, the poet continued to l'Isle-sur-la-Sorgue, where he spent a week (September 7–13, 1950) with his new "God,"[1] René Char. Upon Camus's recommendation Sénac had begun, since November 1949, corresponding with Char in order to publish a few of his poems in *Empédocle* (as we saw previously). Meeting the famous poet was beyond his imagination, part of the traditional ritual of a novice writer visiting an admired master. Not only was he enraptured by his words, noting every behavior of his, he idolized him to the point of keeping the wrappers of Char's favorite candies.[2] Char-Camus, this twin and now close couple, were from then on a highly prized pair of godfathers. Sénac remained faithful to them, despite the winding paths whose twists would necessarily lead to transformations, misunderstandings, conflicts, and sometimes separation.

Sénac arrived in Paris in mid-September, welcomed by Camus, who had returned on the 14th. "Dawn is rising" for the poet, as Camus had underlined in the signed copy of Arthur Rimbaud's *Complete Works* (collection "Pléiade") he had given him on September 15. The "big brother"[3] helps him financially by finding him a job, which would cover his hotel and his daily expenses. His friendship opens the doors to the capital's literary and artistic circles. Until the end of December 1950, Sénac lives happily in the Latin Quarter, sees the writer often, and mingles with his friends and acquaintances (his "gang," his "space") as well as his family. Camus, always kind to him, oversees a show on "The paintings of Sauveur Galliéro and *Soleil*, the literary review of Algiers" (September 2–December 13, 1950) at the Parisian bookstore "73" (73, Boulevard Saint-Michel). The review was experiencing all kinds of difficulties, which Sénac was aware of through the other founding members who had stayed in Algeria.

On the creative level, and with Camus's encouragement, Sénac becomes interested in theater, but fails in his attempts to write, to publish, and to direct,[4] contrary to his famous friend. He was encouraged to publish *Arbre* with Vineta editions, directed by Jean Daniel[5] in Paris. This collection of poems, prefaced by Char,[6] was described as "beautiful" by Camus in a letter he sent to the poet on April 27, 1951. The project, considerably expanded, would later be published as *Poèmes* (as we will see). As proof of his gratitude, Sénac worked on another collection of poems called *Fortifications pour vivre* [Fortifications to live] during his stay in Paris. This collection of poems, abandoned and unpublished for a long time[7]—close to the inspiration of the previous poems (the nobility of suffering engendered by the solitude of flesh, notably in his love for Michèle Ombla, his "mythical fiancée," as he mentioned to Char[8])—was entirely devoted to his two godfathers ("To Albert Camus and René Char, respect and gratitude").

. . .

In January 1951, Camus leaves Paris for Cabris in order to dedicate himself entirely, during a whole semester, to the writing of *L'Homme revolté* [*The Rebel*]. Sénac feels abandoned by a father (they are thirteen years apart) who shortly thereafter would call him *hijo mio* (my son, in Spanish).[9] If Camus experiences towards him, as he himself acknowledged, the "complex of the father,"[10] then wouldn't the son discover in his elder his own image in which he recognizes and loves himself? Whether a presumed or alleged father, a sorcerer or a spiritual father, the reciprocal empathy where the familiar "tu" was never used could only produce inevitable and complex conflicts.

After Camus's departure, the "orphaned" Sénac led a bohemian life in Paris. Without work or resources, he managed to find a job as a caretaker at the "Hostel for Horticultural Apprentices" in Versailles.[11] He informed Camus and also expressed his bitterness. Despite his busy schedule,[12] the "father" answers him in Paris on April 27, 1951, and quickly reprimands him: "You feel that you are being badly treated, while within yourself you were treating others poorly." Paradoxical personality, that of Sénac's, endowed with a powerful ego, demanding and uncompromising toward his friends, but avoiding any responsibility towards them, following an old human law! His temperament didn't hinder him from expressing great "fraternal" generosity toward others: had he not continued, ever since his collaboration with the review *Afrique*, to help and "create," i.e., to promote and give work to young poets and artists? For example, he sends to *Soleil* texts by important authors (René Char, Jean Grenier, Jean Cayrol) for publication, in hopes that the review will gain audience and subscriptions.

In the same letter, Camus writes that he is "all alone with too many things to take care of. Up to now I haven't found any help." An obvious allusion to his life, and in particular to the project of *The Rebel*, which came out in 1951,[13] and which Sénac knew about since he had already published excerpts of it!

As a matter of fact, issue 5 of *Soleil* from February 1951 had featured an essay titled "Les remparts du monde [The ramparts of the world]," signed by Albert Camus (and illustrated with a drawing by Jean de Maisonseul), which was seen as "an unpublished chapter of *The Rebel*, following *The Myth of Sisyphus*."[14] Considering that this essay was for Camus the start of a new cycle, rather than a continuity, one wonders how the review—i.e., Sénac—obtained information that Camus had mentioned to Jean Grenier in 1942.[15] And more importantly, how was Sénac given the privilege, with other rare and prestigious review editors[16]—never mentioned!—to pre-publish, well before *Les Temps modernes* in 1951, revised excerpts (a few variations and a more concise style) that were entirely incorporated by Camus in the chapter "The Sons of Cain."[17]

Perhaps this was the piece that Camus had promised to Sénac in his letter from August 12, 1950. It's difficult to confirm, but the working papers published by *Soleil* are most probably from Char's typed manuscript. The only proof of this theory is the reference edition for the essay, where we see *firsthand* that the typed variations of Char[18]—who was closely associated with the essay's draft—correspond perfectly to the version published by *Soleil*. This brings about another question: Char didn't have the entire manuscript (he received handwritten excerpts as they were being written) until July 12, 1951,[19] five months after the publication of the excerpts in *Soleil*. The mystery regarding the origin of the text published by Sénac therefore remains: was it Camus or Char?

Right after the controversy surrounding *The Rebel*—which followed the polemic with André Breton on Lautréamont[20] in October–November 1951 (the surrealist writer was questioning the essayist's choices and poetic taste)—Sénac resolutely defended Camus in two "open letters" addressed to Breton (whom he met briefly in the Latin Quarter in 1950). "It's regrettable that harsh words can project such stark contrasts between two men that I hold in such high esteem" (first letter). "One need only reread Camus's work, from *Nuptials* to *State of Siege*, to notice the importance he gives to passionate lyricism. But his lucidity—and this explains the myth of Camus's dislike for poetry—is what makes him dissatisfied with false poets, most of those that we admire today" (second letter).[21]

Sénac also sided with his friend against Jean-Paul Sartre, criticizing existentialism ("a philosophy of despair") since 1946, the year of his meeting with Simone de Beauvoir in Algiers.[22] He expressed his unconditional support in a letter to Char, who answered on November 20, 1951: "I'm glad that you sensed the importance of *The Rebel* so strongly. My solidarity with Camus concerning his book is fundamentally unshakable. Camus is manifest integrity" (manifest underlined).[23] This private document is priceless given that Char never spoke out or acted publicly on his friend's behalf during the whole controversy. The letter was so significant that it somewhat altered, for two years,[24] the friendship between Char and Sénac: the first resented that the second had included passages, without his agreement, in his commentary on Camus's essay, published in *La Révolte en question* [The question of rebellion], a special issue of the review *Le Soleil Noir/Positions*.[25] In a response to a questionnaire that often "opposes" Camus, Sénac—considering that "'absolute Rebellion' is a catch phrase, a gut concept"—counters:

> And it's why, as a Christian, furiously Christian, Christian against myself, I am in hopeful communion with the godless man who could write things so beautifully fraternal (followed by long citations of *The Rebel*).[26]

He concludes with observations regarding the critique of Lautréamont, Sade, and Rimbaud, noted by Camus: "Poetry is not the legacy of a few but the wonderful and multiple struggle of all . . ." Poetry does not limit itself to an individualist, intellectual, and interior knowledge, but constitutes also a "national self" in which the poet manifests everyone's alterity within his own ego. This became a constant opposition within Sénac's own self: a poet with an exalted and all knowing "I" who wants to be heard by all citizens. It's the classic idea of poetry as a form of knowledge, renewed here in an ideological weaving that was not yet explicitly proclaimed.

After finishing his essay, Camus returns to Paris on July 12, 1951, and writes to Sénac the very next day in order to renew their friendship and clear up their previous misunderstanding. He informs him that "The Rockefeller Institute in New York is offering travel grants to young Algerian intellectuals," and that he had given his name to Jean Grenier, who was in charge of the operation. Grenier informed Sénac on August 20, 1951,[27] that he wasn't considered because "the R. Foundation is only interested in indigenous [applicants]" [*sic*]—the term "Algerian" wasn't yet applied to the still "indigenous" native population, given the historical context.

Both compassionate and rigorous, Camus wants to "dispel a slight misunderstanding," typical term that was perfectly suited for a son who had already . . . rebelled. "I know what your life is like, and that it's not easy. Nevertheless you are privileged, as I was in Prague. There are difficult privileges." This last sentence was curiously repeated, entirely, and without any mention of its author, in Sénac's manifesto *Le Soleil sous les armes* [*The Sun under the Weapons*].[28] The essay was published in the thick of the Algerian War and contributed greatly to the division between the two men.

Sénac tries to see Camus again during his brief stay in Paris. In a short letter dated July 25, 1951—which he signs with "your friend" for the first and only time—Camus tells him: "Unfortunately I leave tonight and won't be back until around September 10." Exhausted by the new controversy around *The Rebel*, initiated by *Les Temps Modernes*, the writer joins his family in Chambon-sur-Lignon (Haute-Loire)—a center of Protestantism and of the French Resistance against Nazism—leaving Sénac without a place for vacation and increasingly alone.

■   ■   ■

On November 18, 1951, on the eve of an unexpected trip to Algiers, Camus, "a little anxious for many reasons,"[29] sends to Sénac a text without further explanation, which we shall return to later on. In a short accompanying note he specifically insists: "if you retype it, please keep a copy for me," which shows the great trust Camus had in Sénac, who saw this fleeting yet affectionate father less and less in Paris in 1952. Yet, they were connected in their convictions and in their similar tastes, i.e., a concept of life encompassed by the ten keywords—with the exception of "desert"— that were part of Camus's personal mythology and his work: "world, pain, earth, mother, men, desert, honor, misery, summer and sea."[30]

■   ■   ■

Tired of living in misery ("I talk a lot about my clothes / but I have only a jacket / and my meals are scarce . . ."[31]), the poet decided in September 1952 (already planned and mentioned in his letters to Camus and to others in 1950) to return to Algeria—called back, as he often told his friends.

In Algiers, living again in Bab-el-Oued [neighborhood of Algiers], Sénac writes to Camus concerning two projects that would involve him considerably: the publication of *Poèmes*, left in his good care, and a literary review that Sénac wanted to launch in 1953 with funds he inherited from an uncle.

With regard to Sénac's poetry collection, Camus followed every step in the editorial process. In a letter on October 31, 1952, he responded that he was still waiting "for some news regarding the collection. I reviewed it and requested its publication. But we need a second reader, as you know . . . Therefore, let's wait." The review committee at Gallimard[32] included many well-known figures of the time, including Camus; it was therefore extremely difficult for a young writer to pass the committee's ultimate test. In a letter on February 21, 1953, Camus announced that "Your book was accepted, after a few (long) hesitations. I included it in my collection."

This crucial help, which Sénac never ceased to mention, continued since Camus took personal interest in the operations. On November 26, 1953, he wrote: "I was told that your poems will be published in the spring (April May). It's a good time of year to bloom." Sénac waited until June 1954 for his official debut in literature.

As for the review, Camus outlines his contribution in two areas, in a letter from October 30, 1952:

- a literary contribution: in response to Sénac's request, he promises that he'll "send him a text, of course."
- editorial suggestions, and he wonders: "Why the NRA,[33] since you don't want to ape Paris?"* Sénac took this observation into account by removing the title from the editorial manifesto and kept it as a subtitle to his review, now called *Terrasses*. Camus also advises him to "beware of two dangers: 'literature' around the Mediterranean (not too much) and political 'colonialization,' whether direct or indirect, of the Right or of the Left." While this last suggestion is legitimate coming from a writer on the Left "despite myself and against her [the Left],"[34] his questioning of the *Mare nostrum*, a literary myth from his early writings and editorial activities in Algiers,[35] is fairly disconcerting.

At the end of his letter, Camus mentions that the issue would need further discussion during his visit to Algiers in late November.

The writer arrived in Algeria on December 1, 1952. He visited several towns in the South (Djelfa, Ghardaïa, Laghouat, which inspired the novel *The Adulterous Woman*[36]), and was back in Algiers on December 18. On December 21, he signed the editorial manifesto of *Terrasses*, as did the members of the editorial

---

* Alluding to the fact that Sénac is copying the NRF [*Nouvelle Revue Française*].

committee and a few others.[37] Written by Sénac, but revised and supplemented by all the editors, it "hopes to convey the specific testimonial" of Algeria, "one of the richest crucibles of contemporary literature," and to "extricate man from his despair." Sénac found in Camus a project manager whose collaboration would be crucial to the success of the publication, both through his advice and written contributions.

Camus's orientations and inputs were multiple. Sénac gives an enthusiastic account to his friend Mohamed Dib (whom he met at Sidi Madani), in a letter on December 24, 1952:[38]

> We spoke at great length with Camus, during his stay here, concerning the new review. It will be called *Terrasses*. You know our agenda. There will be texts of foremost importance, a sort of "Journal of many voices" edited by all of us, and important chronicles on the growing "Mediterranean" literature (North Africa, Egypt, Palestine, Greece, Lebanon, Spain, Italy, Yugoslavia, etc. . . .), and South American literature. Camus recommended a few chroniclers from those countries. Other than that, I think that Grenier will "cover" Philosophy, Jean Daniel the novels, J.-C. Brieville theater. Camus is also asking that we offer a chronicle to Nicola Chiaromonte, and he himself will contribute regularly to our "Journal." His first text will likely be a novella on Laghouat. He was going to offer *Retour sur l'Homme Révolté* [Return to the Rebel] (with adjustments after controversy) but finally decided to delay its publication.

These last passages show, once more, how informed Sénac was on Camus's literary projects. They also demonstrate without a doubt the latter's crucial role in the review's ambitious editorial line, for a heterogeneous review that brought together his friends and aesthetic concerns that Sénac shared entirely. The review was a major component in the correspondence between the two men in 1953.

Thus upon their return to France, the Camus couple—through Francine, and on the back of her husband's calling card—sent their best wishes to Sénac for the success of his review in January 1953.

In another letter dated February 12, 1953, Camus conveys some of his thoughts on the summary, which "seems good." He comes back to his participation, and announces that he will be submitting an essay, "Retour à Tipasa [Return to Tipasa]." He had revisited the site during his stay in December 1952, probably with Sénac, who also mentioned it.[39] The writer furthermore provides priceless information—impossible to find elsewhere—on the making of a text of crucial importance in the trajectory of the old and new Camus. Concerned as he was with his own legacy, he writes to Sénac: "If you can wait a few days, I will give you a fairly long text (a dozen pages typed), 'Retour à Tipasa,' that I prize and that also takes a 'position' albeit in a purely literary fashion. I'm working on it now."

This correspondence ultimately informs us on the nature of Camus's text, dated November 18, 1951. The writer in fact asks Sénac to return to him "the manuscript of my piece on Char, which you kept. A small German press asked me for a short introduction on Char and I might find a few elements there."[40] This information thus answers the question, raised previously, especially since it is further corroborated by Sénac in a statement that leaves little room for doubt: "Camus . . . once offered me the text, which remains unpublished, for a show that he wrote on René Char upon France's Liberation [in fact, in 1948]."[41] When comparing this original text—entirely edited since then[42]—with Camus's preface, one notices that he pulled from it certain ideas and expressions. Sénac used a few himself, without referencing them, in his commentaries on Char's poetry.[43]

Sénac's eagerness concerning "Retour à Tipasa" causes Camus to write him an unusually caustic letter (envelope dated March 3, 1953): "I was almost going to call to tell you to *leave me alone* as one might say to friends who don't understand that I'm working for them." Exasperated, he adds: "Ah! How I dislike working for reviews, even Algerian ones," a surprising statement coming from the journalist he had always been.

Upon completion of his piece, rewritten four times and finally sent on March 5, 1953, Camus adds: "I would have rewritten it again, if I had the time." "Retour à Tipasa" was in fact reworked, since the version later published as a volume[44] is slightly different than the one published in *Terrasses*[45]—seldom mentioned[46]—in June 1953.

After the issue's release, Camus—very tired—sends a typed letter to Sénac, dated July 3, 1953, and notices that "*Terrasses* presents itself well . . . The first issue is really satisfying." Aside from his essay, the summary is indeed exceptionally coherent. It features a mosaic of authors and texts (prose, poems, book and film reviews, chronicles on Spain and Italy). Next to French authors from France (Francis Ponge, Émile Dermenghen, etc. . . .) we can identify—according to the categories of the time—"Algerians," i.e., French born in Algeria (or having lived there for a long time, such as Gabriel Audisio or Max-Pol Fouchet), foreign natives (Jean Sénac, Jean Daniel, Emmanuel Roblès, etc.), and "indigenous" natives whether they be Arab (Mohamed Dib, Kateb Yacine, Abdelkader Safir) or Berber (Mouloud Feraoun). The latter weren't yet considered as . . . Algerians for reasons that we won't go into here.

This excellent issue is well received by several prestigious literary reviews in France (for example *La Nouvelle Nouvelle Revue Française*, and the *Cahiers du Sud*[47]), as well as by the Algerian press, across party lines. The only exceptions, for political reasons, were on the left (*Alger Républicain*, July 8, 1953) and in a bimonthly review issued by the Algerian Association of Muslim Ulemas [Association des Oulémas musulmans d'Algérie] (*Le Jeune Musulman*, no. 24 from June 26, 1953). The first called for a greater "commitment"—following the Marxist creed—in opposition to the "convoluted and decadent literature" in most texts; the second accepted the designation "Algerian" only "if they follow the actual natural order in Algeria, according to its true representation," alluding to the review of André Chouraqui's book *Les Juifs d'Afrique du Nord* [The Jews of North Africa][48] by Jacques Lévy, considered too biased. Nevertheless in his own mind—and the wording of the review's editorial line leaves no doubt—Sénac envisioned *Terrasses* as a foray into the public debate, aside from action. Literature was poised to enter the political arena.

CHAPTER 4

Towards a Political Literature

E ven though he was concerned about the realities of colonialism, which he regularly denounced under the pseudonym Christian Pérez[1] in both published and unpublished[2] writings, Sénac gave to *Terrasses* a purely literary impulse. His friends, especially Camus, were reluctant and didn't want to overly "politicize"[3] Algerian literature. Camus, who had always acted on behalf of the political liberation of North African nationalist movements, was paradoxically not in support of political literature in Algeria. Perhaps he feared the governor-general of Algeria, whose interventionism had caused him trouble in 1940. But true to himself—upon completion of his review's first issue (which had kept him busy the first semester of 1953)—Sénac renewed his contacts with the Algerian national movements, including militants from the MTLD (Mouvement pour le Triomphe des Libertés Démocratiques/Movement for the Triumph of Democratic Freedoms) and the PPA (Parti du Peuple Algérien/Party of the Algerian People). While remaining sentimentally loyal to his community of origin, mainly through his liberal friend Jean de Maisonseul (whom he had known since 1946), Sénac was in contact with Layachi Yaker, Mohamed Lebdjaoui, Mustapha Kateb,[4] Amar Ouzegane, and even more so with the future

FLN fighters Mustapha Bouhired (Djamila Bouhired's parent) and Mohamed Larbi Ben M'hidi. He would then remain faithful to all of those who shaped him politically in his poetic *romanceros*, meeting them often at Café La Marsa, a nationalist[5] hotbed that belonged to the Ouzegane, also frequented by . . . Albert Camus during his brief stays in Algiers.

While they had common friends in two communities that weren't yet on opposite sides, Sénac—unlike Camus, who lived on the margin of the "Arabs"[6]—was the careful witness of an Algerian reality that he saw daily through its "working class,"[7] a very different reality than that of the colonial order. Under such circumstances, Sénac's humanist sensibility quickly became militant, turning him into a shrewd visionary of the great transformation that was in the making.[8] After the aesthetic Algeria represented in *Soleil* (and to a lesser degree in *Terrasses*), Sénac put forth a plan of action for the birth of an Algerian native homeland, with a first series of poems titled *Matinale de mon peuple* [Dawn of my people] (1949–1953).[9] These ten texts provide luminous clarity on the evolution of the author's growing consciousness.

The title of the first text, "Matinale de mon peuple," implies the choice of a new community other than the original. The poem was followed by a plan of action predicting that "soon the steel will reject the throat," in other words, the end of one world and the forceful emergence of another. Its publication in the first issue of the anticolonial review *Consciences algériennes*,[10] directed by André Mandouze in Algiers, could be seen as a first offensive strategy to translate an ideological rift. In "Les Dormeurs, Honte Honte Honte [The sleepers, shame shame shame]" (the original title for the two poems was "Algérie 1953") and "Faits divers [Random news]," the poet condemns the misery of the men and women around him and proclaims his total devotion:

> you will open your heart to the shared homeland / or you will flee / There's no room for cowards on this earth / and the sun itself is as blunt as a fist [for] the night growls and we are standing to testify . . . / Until the coming of good and honest men.

In "Au pas lent des caravanes [In the slow footsteps of the caravans]"[11] and "Les Belles Apparences [The pretty appearances]," Sénac—reusing the famous "triptych of the palm tree, the woman and the camel," condemned by Robert Randau—chastises an exotic Algeria of clichés ("Madame moukère" [possibly a reference to an Algerian prostitute]), and a touristic Algeria where "people die in silence." While political anger is mounting in an Algeria defined by the "quiet struggles in our veins," Sénac doesn't forget to claim "The rights of love." Revolution and love must first be reconciled. Such a project seemed unrealistic to Camus, who considered that "revolution and love . . . were incompatible."[12] Sénac's tragic destiny would prove him right.

The poem "Les Massacres de Juillet [The massacres of July]" was inspired by a tragic event in Paris. An event that Sénac and Camus experienced differently, foreshadowing the nature of their future positions on the Algerian problem. During a demonstration organized by the MTLD on July 14, 1953, on Place de la Nation, six Algerian workers and one French worker were gunned down by the security forces. While Camus reacts in a letter to *Le Monde* (which speaks of a "skirmish"[13]), wishing for an investigation other than the official one, and condemning a "racism that cannot speak its name," Sénac sees those workers as friends who were part of his "people," even of his "race." "The Arab" is therefore not just the "other," for whom Camus feels offended and wants to defend, but he's an alter ego who like him demands justice.

Finally, the last two poems, "Le Temps des mots [The time for words]," and "Compagnons," evoke the comrades and "the imprisoned homeland," as well as the underground activities of revolutionary militants.

Sénac is well aware, in this summer of 1953, of the evolving national reality in Algeria—which he didn't owe to Camus, as some have hastily suggested[14]— and tries to inform the writer that networks of combatants were ready to start a revolution.[15] Camus denies this, and ironically, on the back of a postcard stamped in Paris on August 29, 1953, he writes: "Do not think too much of the *maquis*.* It's easier to dream of it than to return from it, or even to see it coming." Camus's somewhat unorthodox statement is surprising (the postcard wasn't in an envelope) since it was more public than private (any indiscrete

---

* Term used during WWII to describe the mountains where the French resistance fighters had fled in order to fight against German occupation. The same word was used during the Algerian War, in reference this time to the Algerian resistance fighters against France.

viewer would have understood the severity of the message, given the context). This political difference didn't keep Camus from being a loyal North African. He expressed his support by intervening on the behalf of militant Algerians (November 26, 1951) and Tunisians (April 12, 1954) who had come into conflict with the colonial law.[16]

On the literary end, Camus requests an update on *Terrasses*, on November 26, 1953, hoping that "the second issue will come out." As we know, the review had only a single issue, the second issue never making it beyond the proofs, for lack of money (and discipline from its director). The adventure came to a halt despite several attempts by Sénac and his friends to restart it in Algiers,[17] and later in Paris.

The year 1954 was pivotal for Sénac, both in terms of his entry into the literary world, thanks to Camus, and in terms of his now obvious support of an *Algerian* Algeria. On this issue, his disagreement with Camus deepens in the following months, even though he continues to admire him on the literary end. The poet maintains an unstable equilibrium, speaking of Camus with "fervor, anger, lightness and affection, and admiration"[18] with friends they had in common. He doesn't yet understand Camus's modest attitude (which others, including Sénac, later called "silence") towards the irreversible rise of Algerian nationalism, including early warning signs that went beyond the simple "language of hate."[19] This was all the more painful for Sénac, who had not only unequivocally chosen a people and a homeland—though both still hypothetical—but also a "new" Algeria for the Berber and Arab Algerians. The pages of his *Journal* are eloquent on this issue, which he describes as "the crux of my daily life."[20]

Contrary to the unanimous consensus of his community of origin, which he had not yet relinquished, the poet no longer hides his "national (Algerian[21]) opinions" and resolutely sides with "the cause of the Arabs, our Cause."[22] One would have to quote entire passages of Sénac's *Journal* to understand his foreboding and lucid vision concerning the future of this "Mother Algeria," which he called a "total sacrifice." The following passages are entirely proven in historical hindsight:

> [The] Europeans from here . . . too certain of their racial superiority . . . must face the facts and be given the following choice: Algeria or departure . . . I don't

believe in anything other than a radical revolution, for the future and for the greatness of this country.[23]

Although Sénac's commitment certainly leaves no doubt, the poet still has the linguistic mannerisms of typical French Algerians, sometimes calling his people "Arabs." This wasn't a derogatory term, since they defined themselves as such,[24] and yet, Sénac would later criticize its use by Camus.

Despite their obvious political differences, still private in nature, Sénac doesn't forget Camus. In February 1954, Sénac informs him—after Roblès—that the governor-general was implicated in the Algerian Novel Prize (Prix Algérien du Roman), which Jean Pomier wanted to establish in Paris.[25] Camus copies Pomier, on February 26, 1954, a letter announcing his withdrawal from the jury, and in another letter on March 2, 1954, he gives important information concerning his public and private connections in Algeria:

> I thought that it was about literature. The least one can say is that it's not entirely clear . . . I'm worried that by removing myself from the jury I will upset a lot of good people, but I do so without hesitation.

In his letter he also states that he should have "limited himself to information" and not some kind of "denunciation," a word "that none of you have the right to use . . . Tell it clearly to all of our comrades." Camus never ceased to act as a true spiritual advisor, if not as an enlightened facilitator towards his circle of Algerian writers who always listened to him, and whom he always privileged, according to Lottman.[26]

After the publication of *L'Été*,[27] Sénac again expresses his enthusiasm and writes the following entry in his journal on April 7, 1954:

> I feel like I can understand Camus, penetrate his imperfections, love him. He's at the stake, he who listens and screams: "Father," burned by despair and pride, and already saved by love.[28]

Sénac's dualist vision of Camus becomes clearer. He views positively the writer of a "sensitive" Algeria, whose texts are relatively old (six out of eight are prior to 1953). He also becomes exasperated since the buds of the rebellion are so obvious (to him, the insider) and bewildered by the obstinate short-sightedness of the man who should have noticed them, since he had studied them in the '40s in his articles for *Alger Républicain* and *Combat.*

Sénac is so delighted with Été that he dedicates an entire show to the collection, titled "Table Ronde sur *L'Été* [Panel discussion on *L'Été*],"[29] on April 14, 1954, with Edmond Brua, Sauveur Galliéro—friends in common with Camus—and El Boudali Safir, who was in charge of the Muslim programs on Radio Alger. Following a more general discussion (situating the text within Camus's larger work, and the recurrent theme opposing justice and freedom), Sénac rightly considers that his "texts on Oran and the 'cities without a past' are unfair." Without challenging it, he disapproves of the vision of a man rooted exclusively in the classical European culture, who disregards the other dimension of Algerian civilization that is not just French (suggested in undertone) and that is ultimately "searching for a solution away from the nihilism" analyzed in *The Rebel.* Camus would continue his pursuit in intersecting art and politics—which Sénac had detected in its premises—throughout the Algerian War, in journalistic writings that would greatly anger the poet, who was vigilant even though he might have been a neophyte.

Finally, in his highly ideological prose text "La Patrie,"[30] which he began in March 1954, Sénac includes a statement by Napoléon Bonaparte from Camus's "Les Amandiers": "Did you know, Napoléon asked Fontanes, what I admire most in the world? It is the impotence of force when it comes to founding something, etc." But Sénac, in another one of his literary ruses, slightly modifies the text by removing the question mark: "What I admire most in the world is the impotence of force when it comes to founding something," turning its author (intentionally omitted) into a "conqueror." Even though it's for a good cause, Sénac's biased gesture of appropriating a real citation makes it seems apocryphal by significantly modifying its meaning.

The opinions of the two friends are increasingly irreconcilable on the political front. After the fall of Dien-Bien-Phu (May 7, 1954) Camus experiences "[an] ambiguous feeling of shame and horror, like in [19]40,"[31] whereas Sénac remains silent in his journal, expressing his Algerian nationalism in a poem (May 1954) that doesn't hide his anticolonialism:

If to sing my love is to love my homeland / I am a combatant who doesn't repudiate himself.

This would be the poet's leitmotif throughout his life, who doesn't forget—under the circumstances—to evoke "The blood of Dien-Bien-Phu or that of *Casa*."[32] It's again, in this case, the same diptych: Love-Revolution.

Meanwhile, on the literary side—following the publication of his collection *Poèmes* in June 1954—Sénac conveys his "Joy of being with Camus and Char for this new beginning."[33] Prior to his leaving for France, on July 27, 1954, on the eve of a crucial turning point in Algerian history, Sénac writes to Camus: "I embrace you, big serpentine brother," a direct allusion to his friend's art of avoiding politics. He announces that he will arrive in Paris in a month, where he will live thanks to "realist friends" since "it's becoming impossible for me to stay here, I no longer have any real job or home." Refusing to "collaborate with this vast sabotage operation, the negation of the Algerian personality,"[34] he ceases to produce his radio shows with Radio Alger—he had experienced all kinds of obstacles for having condemned the exclusion of Muslim comedians and for having used the term "Algerian fatherland" in reference to Mouloud Mammeri's novel *La Colline oubliée* [The Forgotten Hill].[35]

Sénac also asks Camus for his help in securing an advance payment of 60,000 francs[36] from Gallimard. He finally informs him about his literary projects, which include *Élégies rudérales*, completed, and an essay on Oran, in progress: "Oran ou les statues sous la peau [Oran or the statues under the skin]." The elegies would be partially included in the collection *Les Désordres* [The disorders], dedicated to Camus.[37] The essay, published in two different versions,[38] was a variation on *Le Minotaure ou la Halte d'Oran*,[39] which Sénac had praised as "pure poetry, after a few lucid and pointed remarks."[40] A comparative reading of the two texts would be interesting since they follow an identical narrative structure: elaborating thoughts on the same issue, the absence of "Arab" neighborhoods. Their perspectives on Oran are nevertheless different: critical in Camus's case and hedonistic in the case of Sénac, who denies that it is "the capital of boredom" in his radio show *Oran, our town*.[41] Jean Paulhan accurately distinguished the two, in a letter he sent to the poet from October 12, 1954:

I enjoyed its warmth and surprises, while at times I found you a little insistent and monotonous.[42]

André Bélamchi, a specialist on Federico Garcia Lorca from Oran, who knows both the poet and the writer, even finds that Sénac's text is more "beautiful" than Camus's.[43]

In his answer by postcard on August 9, 1954, Camus warns Sénac against coming to Paris without any guarantees and seems doubtful as to whether Gallimard will grant him any advance, which the poet did eventually get thanks to his support.[44] The seemingly reserved attitude of the writer, who was experiencing difficulties in his marriage at the time, contrasts significantly with the help he provided Sénac in his travel projects, four years earlier.

On August 29, 1954, Sénac landed in Paris, on a flight from Oran. A new chapter was about to begin, one in which Sénac's political activism—which was already distancing him from Camus—would eventually bring about the end of their friendship.

PART II

Literature between Rebellion and Revolution (1954–1958)

CHAPTER 5

November 1954: The "Just" Fight or Terrorism?

Following a short trip to Northern France with some friends, Sénac returns to Paris on September 15, 1954. He's again close to Camus, whom he sees almost every day, and who starts calling him "son." The poet is so touched that he strives, in his writing, to shape his quest for a father, or at least to provide a sketch of it [in his autobiographical novel *Ébauche du père*]. "For such a long time I have been speaking from my mother's womb,"[1] [he writes]. He emphasizes his Spanish origins, and like Camus, Sénac might have said, "In my blood, Spain is my second fatherland,"[2] even though their lineages were different.[3] Sénac did say of Camus, "The sun of Africa and the cruel blood of Spain," shedding additional light on their distinctive perspectives.[4]

In Camus, Sénac had undeniably found the substitute father whom he had often looked for since adolescence in diverse and dissimilar figures, such as Brua or Randau. There are many accounts of this, either from friends like Jules Roy ("Camus had for the lively Sénac the affection of a father towards a son"[5]), or from Sénac's own account.[6]

As in every filial relationship, the "son" remains obedient to the prodigal "father," who gives him his undivided attention even with the occasional outbursts due to the poet's temperament. Thus, on October 11 and 18, 1954, Camus "firmly" advises Sénac to stay in Paris even though he had received an interesting offer from Radio Algérie.[7] Despite the worries caused by his wife's illness and his nagging inability to write ("barren for ten months"), Camus, in a letter to Sénac on November 12, expresses his happiness with the *Times*'s favorable review of the *Poèmes* collection, "which is selling well."[8] Furthermore, on the eve of his departure for Italy, on November 22, and again upon his return, on December 22, Camus provides concrete help to the poet: he requests that Suzanne Agnely supply him with 15,000 francs.

Their disagreement nevertheless intensifies on the political front, without affecting their friendship yet. Following Sénac's meeting with François Mauriac at the *Figaro* headquarters on October 20, 1954, to inform him of an imminent armed "insurrection" in Algeria against colonial France, he is criticized by Camus for his "acquaintance"[9] with the "Dostoevsky of the Gironde."[10] The Algerian War erupts on November 1, 1954. Even if the two friends respond to the event as French Algerians, using similar vocabulary, they show stark differences in their political opinions. Sénac's *Carnet* [Notebook] from that period (November–December 1954)[11] reveals itself as a crucial document concerning their first "heated" reactions.

For the author of *The Rebel*—who nine years earlier had warned against the "inferior position of the Muslim people" of Algeria, but who nevertheless believed that they had to be "conquered a second time" (even if "the era of imperialism is past")[12]—a war seemed improbable, if not inconceivable, since it was only an issue of "terrorism." Terrorism "preoccupies" him, writes Sénac on November 3, "but he condemns the crimes of political cowards and accepts only the terrorism of *The Just* (Kaliayev, Russia, 1905)." The play, which questions the justification of political murder and of violent revolutionary action, provides a particular echo given the circumstances. Under the colonial system of Algeria—unjust for Camus, dominating and repressive for Sénac—is it possible to kill without hatred, for an idea, especially those who are innocent? (In Camus's play, inspired by a historical event, the Grand Duchess Catherine and particularly the two children are the innocent victims of on an assassination attempt on the Grand Duke Serge, uncle of the czar and governor of Moscow, as they were riding in his carriage. The *grand-duc* was eventually killed in Moscow, on February 17, 1905, by an "organization" sometimes called "Socialist Revolutionary Party"). Their responses to this issue would determine their respective positions on the Algerian War. Camus's position, which is well known, will be presented here in opposition to Sénac's actions and responses.

Concerning the concepts of violence and justice, Camus always positions himself strictly on the moral, if not sentimental plane. In *The Just*, for example, "the delicate murderer" Kaliayev is willing to die for the crime he committed, so that his own death preserves the law of retaliation and turns his assassination into an act of justice. Camus, who didn't subscribe to this attitude, expresses on November 3, 1954 (as told by Sénac) a position that would remain unchanged. He categorically and unequivocally condemns the violence of terrorism, which he saw as implicitly that of the "Arabs."

For Sénac, considering his prior intuitions, apprehensions, and even certainties, this "terrorism" represents a new historical reality as revolutionary. Rejecting blind violence on both sides, he nevertheless understands the violence of the Algerian fighters as long as they can avoid a "reverse racism," by protecting "the lives of others" and by "striking only the heads." Also, in opposition to Camus's law of retaliation (a life for a life) and true to himself, he wonders whether the "time has come to live (and to die)" for his "carnal homeland," and dreams of an "international brigade" that would fight alongside the "North African terrorists and speed up the people's liberation" (*Carnets* [Notebooks], November 4). But he doesn't yet know how, or where, to act and/or write to that effect. In November 1954, the "rebel ready to become a revolutionary" was ultimately not Camus, as Jean Grenier had thought,[13] but Sénac. As in the play *The Just*, Kaliayev-Camus will struggle with his antithesis Stepan-Sénac, a tireless activist who is concerned mostly with efficiency and not with politico-ideological rhetoric, no matter how meticulous. The test of war would ultimately prove him right.

Sénac writes on December 15 that he plans to dedicate himself "entirely" to his "People," to his "Algerian homeland," without betraying his conscience as a "Frenchman" who loves "Arabs." His friendship with Camus lives on. The twenty-eight-year-old son still admires his father, who just turned forty-one and who remains "bigger, straighter, purer, warmer than ever" (November 12, 1954). Sénac isn't yet ranting against the real man, who thinks that the poems of *Matinale de mon peuple* are "good" and who even gets Gallimard's agreement to have them published elsewhere.[14] This came as a marvelous surprise to the poet, who, while he admits to lying in his more personal texts,[15] accepts no criticism[16] and gives considerable credit to his own political texts, as in the following excerpt of his *Carnets*, dated November 17:

> The author doesn't subscribe to any party. He simply wants to give the account
> of a young Algerian intellectual who's witnessing his country's misfortune.

Politically mature, Sénac decides to puts his faith into a cause that he believes is right instead of opting for a dogmatic militancy. Such a position, purely humanist in nature, could be motivated in part by his religious ethics (guilty Catholic pity and its corollary, solidarity). Nevertheless, the subtle relational dialectic between Sénac and Camus (the yet undeclared opposition to the war that was starting at home, on one hand; on the other, the reciprocal affection of two men where one owed much to the other) cannot last. The poet's attitude becomes quickly and inevitably radicalized.

Starting in January 1955, Sénac mentions in his *Carnet* the "battles" and the "escalation" of the Algerian struggle, and begins to add a little sun with five rays to his signature.[17] His meeting—on January 21, at the Old Navy bar in Saint-Germain-des-Prés—with Ahmed Taleb-Ibrahimi and Layachi Yaker,[18] two militants from the nascent French Federation of the FLN [Fédération de France du FLN], will strengthen his commitment and precipitate his Cornelian tragedy. That same day he writes his first circumstantial and sufficiently explicit pro-Algerian poem, "Les Partisans de l'Aurès,"[19] in which he states:

> War is a folly / we are not violent / and nevertheless mother Algeria / your
> pain makes us mean.

Unlike Camus, who he thought was always hesitating or staying silent on their shared tragedy, Sénac enters the fray and joins the anticolonial resistance once and for all, first in words, then in deeds.

He works tirelessly within the burgeoning French Federation of the FLN: organizing networks, participating in gatherings and strikes, drafting pamphlets, printing the *Bulletin de la Fédération de France du FLN*,[20] then *El Moudjahid*, acting as liaison for FLN-MNA (MNA, National Algerian Movement, rival party founded on December 3, 1954, by Messali Hadj, in fratricidal opposition to the FLN), etc. His actions during the Algerian War (contrary to those of Camus that are well-known) need to be told, given the shadows, and labyrinths they hold; these are partly due to Sénac's need to hide and dispel any suspicion, and partly because some Algerians today tend to minimize these actions, if not ignore them. During his lifetime—aside from a few random notes in notebooks and rough drafts—the poet confided only in a few friends and well-known correspondents. Judge Michelle Beauvillard, advocate for the leaders of the FLN in French prisons, kept documents on Sénac's past actions.

Sénac's militancy will progressively and inevitably generate a conflict with Camus, who nevertheless keeps his trust in him. He proves this, during his visit to Algiers from February 17–March 1, 1955, by quoting him in an interview given to his old friend Edmond Brua, who had become editor in chief of *L'Echo d'Alger*.[21] Without being a dissident, the poet soon calls out Camus upon his return [to Paris]. The son's first rebellion occurs on March 28, when he writes in his first "Notebook":

> After an initial clash and a long discussion, Camus agrees (in the presence of Suzanne Angely and Guilloux) to become publicly and explicitly involved in the Algerian struggle by manifesting his solidarity with Ferhat Abbas.

Then in a second "Notebook," on the same date, he specifies:

> Discussion with Camus and agreement to speak with the Union of Algerian Students [Union des Étudiants Algériens] and to collaborate with the Algerian Republic of Abbas, the Republican . . . You convinced me. Joy, cries of joy. Camus joins us in the struggle . . . Camus who calls himself my Father, my big brother (he combs me, changes my hairstyle, which displeases him), expresses tenderness towards me.[22]

These two writings allow us to draw, aside from confirming the close relationship between the two men, the following hypothesis and conclusion.

First they reveal that Camus had imagined early on a solution, if not a political project, for an Algeria at war, which would be publicly outlined as the situation deteriorated. In the beginning of spring 1955, his solution seems close to that of Ferhat Abbas, who had always advocated for all types of reform on behalf of his community, without putting the French presence in danger. If Sénac refers to this somewhat moderate nationalist leader—having crossed paths with militants of his UDMA party in Algiers since 1950—it was probably not by conviction. Having sided with the FLN's combatant Algeria, it's with political realism that Sénac incites Camus to work at least toward a "broad and profound" transformation. Even though his sympathy for Ferhat Abbas had been proven since May 1945,[23] Camus doesn't consider the possibility of an independent Algeria. Had he not asked Sénac at the time: "And you, do you believe in an independent Algeria?"[24]

But to the great despair of a euphoric Sénac—who had considered that Camus's new attitude was "the most noble joy" of his life, to the point where he could "now die" with just that one "mission" completed—the promise made by his so-called father would remain unfulfilled.

Two reasons for this can be mentioned:

First of all, Camus temporarily disengaged himself from Algeria in order to focus on his personal projects (the staging of Dino Buzzati's play *Un Cas intéressant* [*Un caso clinico*]) and to travel (Greece and Italy). In addition, as he would tell his friends and loved ones, he believed that Algeria's future depended on the return to power of Pierre Mendès France. Camus would advocate for him in his editorials for *L'Express*, from May 14, 1955, to February 2, 1956, instead of collaborating with *La République algérienne*, the UDMA's press gallery, as he had promised Sénac.

Secondly, whether in Paris or abroad, Camus didn't make contact with Ferhat Abbas in Algiers. Even though the latter's political organization participated in the local Algerian elections, on April 17 and 24—this time with a true desire for independence—the charismatic leader no longer had any faith in a sustained and unrewarded "restraint." He was already in secret negotiations with the FLN, which he would officially join a year later in Cairo, on April 25, 1956.[25]

The meeting with the Algerian students was delayed and would take place only six months later. In the meantime, in 1955, the situation in Algeria had deteriorated: the state of emergency of March 31 was gradually extended to the rest of Algeria; the continuous reinforcement of the military, reaching 100,000 men in May (as opposed to 49,700 in November 1954); the many demonstrations in France of those who were drafted and redrafted (Sénac would have been called had he not been a volunteer during World War II); the massacres and the repressions in Algeria's Nord-Constantinois on August 20; the inclusion—for the first time—of the Algerian problem at the UN's tenth session, on September 30, etc. . . . The war turned into a military and political quagmire. Camus was so worried that he expressed his concern in articles for *L'Express*, and to his friends,[26] including Sénac, who writes on October 4, 1955:

> Camus is ill. Algeria is going to kill us all. "Notebooks, 1955."

As for the poet, he was always on the front lines. In conversation with his "Arab" and *pied-noir* friends, like Emmanuel Roblès, he sees no "solution other than constant rebellion and blood in 'our' Algeria stricken in the sun" (Notebook, September 6, 1955). As the war was deteriorating, the "son" continues to defend a tormented nationalism, and rebels more and more openly against the "father." He does so on October 13, 1955, in the company of their mutual friend André Bélamich,[27] and in November 1955 with four poems from *Matinale de mon peuple* incisively titled "Let's stop the Algerian war,"[28] published in a special edition of *Esprit*.

Sénac, who was given the task of preparing the meeting with the Algerian students (planned for a long time), organized it—by an unfortunate twist of fate—the day after his latest altercation with Camus, on October 14, 1955. Instead of being held in Camus's office at Gallimard, as originally planned,[29] the event took place at *L'Express* in the evening, from 6 to 8:30. Aside from Sénac, the student delegation (all part of the UGEMA*) included its president, Ahmed Taleb-Ibrahimi, as well as Layachi Yaker, Rédha Malek, and Mouloud Belouane.[30] That same day Sénac writes a sober "very good" in his *Journal*, suggesting that the meeting went well (if that's what he's referring to). This

---

* General Assembly of Muslim Algerian Students, founded at the constitutive congress of July 8–14, 1955, in Paris).

wasn't the view shared by Ahmed Taleb-Ibrahimi[31] or by Rédha Malek,[32] who saw Camus as a pragmatist, i.e., doubtful with respect to the national agenda of the Algerian conflict, and clearly differentiating French and Arabs. However the two men provide no further details on the meeting, in terms of its date, and don't mention either that Sénac had called it.

Olivier Todd also speaks of the meeting in his book, but it includes several inaccuracies:[33] it happened at *L'Express* and not in Camus's office at Gallimard, rue Sébastien Bottin; Ahmed Taleb-Ibrahimi never headed the clandestine newspaper *El Moudjahid*: he wasn't in Algiers for the first seven issues, and for the eighth (published in Paris on August 5, 1957,[34] the first time abroad) he was in prison (in Fresnes, since February 26, 1957); finally, Sénac didn't call Camus a coward until later (an incident that we will return to).

Sénac—sole instigator of the meeting, a memorable one for the Algerian side—later wrote to his friend Jean de Maisonseul:

> [It] didn't go well at all. Camus with his irony, his defensive instinct and already his agoraphobia (he wasn't expecting that they would be so many). Camus saying: we'll sit on the ground just like home. On the way out they were all disappointed in their meeting with the great writer.[35]

Ten years later—in an afterword for an unfinished new edition of *Soleil sous les armes*—Sénac again remembered that "secret meeting," marked by the "painful altercation to convince the estranged big 'brother,' surrounded in his proud 'torment.'"[36] As a small comfort, the members of the group ran into Robert Barrat as they were leaving; he had just come back from the Algerian *Maquis* with a famous article "A French journalist with the Algerian 'outlaws,'"[37] which was censored.

The political disagreements between Sénac and Camus on Algeria haven't yet disrupted their friendship. As proof: Camus agrees, on October 20, 1955, to collaborate with *Terrasses*—which the poet is always planning to resurrect ("Notebook 1955")—and indicates, on December 23, that he is favorable to publishing his new collection, *Les Désordres*, which was unanimously accepted at Gallimard (with a few minor comments). But they had to "wait" since the previous book, *Carnet 1955*, was "hardly two years old." On December 29, Camus granted the impoverished Sénac—who spent almost his entire life[38] without resources—20,000 francs in advance, which allowed him to "get a room and find a job again." Sénac writes to his "teacher, friend (despite the thorns)" to thank him for getting him out of a tight spot. He was so happy that he prayed for his protector and his family at Notre-Dame in Paris; "that hadn't happened to me for a long time." "With gratitude and affection," he gives him Char's original letter on *The Rebel*, from November 21, 1951.

These "thorns," in early 1956, appear between two men of Mediterranean temperament (both sang their love for the *Mare Nostrum*) but with different personalities, and seemingly skilled in the art of "false truths" (Sénac becomes truly depersonalized, depending on his interlocutor, taking on multiple identities in his writing and in his life; Camus never writes about what he truly thinks,[39] even though "the Republic of Literature" sees him as a postwar guru). Yet their friendship, which had always been respectful, now becomes oddly ambiguous.

Already, during a verbal dispute on March 28, 1955, Camus had asked Sénac to "humanize their relations," which had become clearly unhealthy. Sénac answered:

> When we meet, we always yell at each other. Our human interactions occur only when we are absent. (*Carnet 1955*)

Here lies the tragic ambivalence: while Sénac worships the man, the writer, the "father" in Camus—to whom he feels most indebted—he's increasingly clashing with his political ideas, which he finds profoundly irritating. The younger is still fascinated by the elder, but he's appalled at his thoughts concerning their native land. Could their friendship be saved? The evolution of the Algerian War, and especially of Camus's opinions, increasingly disturb Sénac, now called a "resolute Scipion"[40] by the author of *Caligula*, who references his own literary works to strengthen his argument. In this play, so close to the Algerian tragedy of the two friends, the young poet Scipion and the philosopher Chaerea—who understood from early on the troubling personality of the Roman emperor Caligula—end up joining those who were conspiring to assassinate the dictator in order to give everyone's life a new meaning.

Sénac's conspiracy against Camus was gradually unfolding, and would be increasingly obvious due to the circumstances of the war and their diverging itineraries.

CHAPTER 6

The Civil Truce

n January 1956, as a leftist government came into power in France and Algeria—elected to make "peace in Algeria," but becoming increasingly hawkish (with both Guy Mollet, president of the Council, and Robert Lacoste, resident minister, elected during the January 2 legislative session)—Camus presented his idea of a civil truce in *L'Express*,[1] while Sénac published his "Letter to a young Frenchman of Algeria" ["Lettre à un jeune Français d'Algérie"] in *Esprit*.[2] A comparative reading of these texts ultimately sheds light on their antagonistic views concerning the Algerian War.

In his articles [in *L'Express*], Camus advocates for a dialogue in order to revitalize the concept of a "Franco-Muslim community," or an approximation thereof, where "French and Arabs are condemned either to live or to die together," where the "French fact" in Algeria is primordial and the "dream of France's disappearance is childish." Camus suggests that the elites of the two predominant groups ("Liberal French" and "Arab democrats") intervene through strong condemnation and through appeasement—to put an end to the "bloody marriage between terrorism and repression"—and refuses all discussion with the "rebel army," believing that they were under Egyptian influence,

as did most of metropolitan France and its governments until 1962.[3] He finally
suggests a political solution close to that of Guy Mollet's triptych (declaration
of February 16, 1956): "cease-fire—elections—negotiations" for an "Algeria
of justice, where French and Arabs can freely associate" in a renewed French
Union incorporated into Europe. Camus would later refine and nuance his
thinking, but for him the fate of Algeria was tied to that of France. It's curious
that the writer, who wanted justice for the Arabs in a French framework, was so
late in joining the supporters of an Algerianist ideology that he opposed; even
its literature, with the exception of Edmond Brua.[4]

In his "Letter to a young Frenchman of Algeria," mainly written between
the 4th and the 15th of January 1956—perhaps as a reply to Camus's articles
in *L'Express*—Sénac displays a political lucidity that Camus was "apparently"
lacking. Without seeing him or even citing him, Sénac confronts him through
the press. Sénac goes further than Camus in his denunciation of the blatant
injustices and the humiliation that the "Arabs" experienced under colonialism—which explained for him the ongoing tragedy (in this sense he joins
Camus on the origin of the war—elevating it to the level of race, and not just
socioeconomics—which the writer had consistently denounced since 1939).
The latter cannot imagine a new Algeria without French and Arabs. The word
choice, neither accidental nor speculative, is a fundamentally political issue.

On that basis the poet begins to analyze the country's reality, i.e., a separation (and not an association), as seen in the following statement: "The game
is over for the masters of Algeria," since "with the Army of National Liberation
(military branch of the FLN), the people of Algeria have won the battle." Despite
"the strength, the repression and the excess of power," the masters won't last
more than "five years maximum," a surprisingly accurate prediction that
was off only by a year (article published in March 1956; signing of the Évian
Accords leading to independence, in March 1962). He believes that the spirit
of Bandung—which freed the people and the weight of an unbearable war for
the French—would contribute to this victory. As for the communal dialogue
that Camus had called for, and the inevitable mutual concessions (but what
could the "Arabs" offer, having so little compared to the "racial privilege" that
Sénac condemned, including that of the "petits blancs" defended by Camus?),
the poet wants them as well, but only within a renewed consciousness and

identity that was freely chosen, a "night of August 4th"—in short, a new era that mirrored the abolition of feudal privileges during the French Revolution of 1789.

The option consists of convincing the French of Algeria, primarily defended by Camus, to "embrace" the independence of Algeria and its predominantly Arabo-Berber-Muslim identity. In accepting a necessarily "minoritarian" position, the Europeans could avoid, if they chose to, the tragic outcome of "the suitcase or the coffin." To his own native countrymen, Sénac suggests a reconciliation that would involve their participation in building a new homeland, a "difficult and unique project" confronted with differences of birth, of languages, of religions, and with the fatal—but temporary—spirit of revenge that the previously oppressed would feel towards their former oppressors, perhaps enemies, if not adversaries. Endowed with political realism that bordered on naive cynicism, Sénac would pay dearly for his militancy in independent Algeria, because of his background and his disarming nonconformity, which would eventually exclude him from the city that he nevertheless helped build.

Thus, in the stances he takes and in the words he uses, the "son" is now publicly in opposition to the discourse of the "father." Even though he doesn't denounce Camus's call for a civil truce in Algiers, on January 22, 1956, he doesn't believe in its chances of success. And there are abundant reasons for his skepticism:

Sénac and Camus both disapprove of violence, no matter where it comes from ("the barbarity of some," the poet observes,[5] "leads to the barbarity of others"; "no death, no matter whose," can please me, says the writer[6] who saw that violence—that of "Arab" terrorism—was indiscriminate, and even acknowledged two years later, in *Actuelles III* (1958), that the Arabs suffered more than the French). But Sénac isn't afraid of clearly condemning the sole culprit, "a certain policy of French occupation that is more or less colonialist, and profoundly racist."[7] While going with Camus's concept of legitimate violence, which was expressed in *The Just*—a play that is symbolically representative of an Algerian War that was a "personal tragedy" for the two friends—Sénac writes the following on the back of an envelope dated "Marseille, December 1955": "Beware, all of our words are accountable. Violence is never right, but it is justified and necessary." As a resistant, Camus had written a similar statement:

"The years of the Occupation have taught me to believe that violence is inevitable."[8] Camus, who could accept the use of violence during French resistance to Nazism, was now against it in Algeria's war, "without understanding its purpose or modalities, or refusing to understand them."[9] For Sénac, the Algerian fighters, who "are backed by the entire Muslim population and by all the official indigenous political figures,"[10] were fighting for the liberation of Algeria. For him it was an anticolonial war—i.e., for another Algerian nation—and not a civil war for a social and economic "shining justice," as it was for Camus.

In his published, unpublished, and private (correspondence) writings, Sénac—a discerning Paladin, as he often was in politics—wholeheartedly supported the FLN's plan, the "only realistic solution,"[11] even though he still considered himself a French Algerian. He goes against Camus, who avoids the issue, and delays "the necessary solutions, even the means to achieve them in order to reconcile the Algerian problem."[12] Did the writer, faced with the deteriorating situation, abandon the idea of a federal republic allied to the French Union, which he defended six months earlier, on July 23, 1955, in the pages of *L'Express*?[13] There's reason to believe it, since that piece isn't included with the other articles in *Actuelles III: Chroniques algériennes*, where Camus chronologically combines his essential political writings on Algeria. Federalism, though, would find there a more precise formulation, which we will address later.

The main organizers of the conference, who call for a civil truce benefiting both sides, are old friends of both Sénac and Camus: Jean de Maisonseul and Emmanuel Roblès, on the "French liberal" side, are seated with Camus; Amar Ouzegane and Mohamed Lebjaoui, on the "Arab democrats" side, remained in the audience.[14] Camus didn't know until then that the latter had been militants within the FLN. He discovered only too late that he was "obligated to the FLN," according to Amar Ouzegane,[15] and that the Cercle du Progrès hall,[16] where the meeting was taking place, was supervised by militants from the Autonomous Area [Zone autonome] of Algiers.[17] Sénac, on the other hand, knew it. He saw them at Café La Marsa. In *Aux héros purs* [To the pure heroes]—which he later dedicated to Ouzegane, minister of agriculture and of the agrarian reform in Algeria's first government after independence (on September 27, 1962)—Sénac recalled "the dreams that we had in the dark and luminous summers at La Marsa—and that our brothers have carried out."[18] Ouzegane, in turn, dedicated *Le Meilleur Combat*[19] to Sénac, recalling "the many evenings spent at the Café of [L]a Marsa on the eve of the Algerian Revolution, where I was admiring the manuscript for the blazing poems in *Matinale de mon peuple* [Dawn of my people]."[20] Finally, ten years later—at the time Visconti's *The Stranger* was being filmed in 1966–1967 (we will return to this later)—several of Camus's friends met with Edmond Charlot and Jean Sénac in Algiers, in the home of Jean de Maisonseul (January 16, 1967), and recalled the civil truce. Sénac summarizes their discussions in his "Notebook,"[21] and mentions Camus's "anger" upon learning that he had been misled by the FLN—the participants at the conference and the militants who were maintaining order. This description contradicts those of the witnesses, who spoke of Camus's rather conciliatory attitude toward his interlocutors during that specific event of the Algerian War.

Sénac, very much informed by his French or Algerian friends who had remained in Algeria, knew through experience that the time for truce had passed. Familiar with the habits and customs of the vast majority of "Pieds-Noirs," who wanted to protect their assets against all odds and were resistant to any dialogue with a Muslim population that was claiming its freedom in open dissidence—and not just more justice (two concepts that Camus tried to reconcile)—he told his friends (and wrote a little later) that Camus's "noble"[22] calls would be ineffective, and that none of the parties would listen, entrenched as they were in their own ghettos (spatial, religious, linguistic, social, and civilizational), so vividly described by the author of *The Stranger* in his fictions. The evil system was relentless, and time would soon prove Sénac right: following the violent demonstrations (the "Day of the Tomatoes" on February 6, 1956), the French of Algeria (the "ultras") forced Guy Mollet to reorient his policy in Algeria to their advantage. The residing Minister Lacoste, appointed on February 9, disregarded Camus's call ("Me, I wage war!")[23] and refused to receive the "very moderate French delegation that came to request that he consider a round table and a Truce, whereas he met every day with extremist delegations of settlers and veterans."[24] It was a stalemate, and Sénac believed that one had to choose "sides," in this case a different side than Camus's since "the only solution consists of negotiating with the heads of the Algerian resistance, as equals."[25]

Finally, even though Camus acknowledges—for the first time since the beginning of the war—the existence of an "Arab movement," described until then as "terrorist" or "invisible enemy," Sénac notes that the speaker focuses primarily on the "million French established in Algeria for the past century,"[26] as did most of the governments and of the French under the Fourth Republic. Sénac, decidedly more in tune with the upheavals of history in the making, suggests that together they build a free Algerian state where, given the same rights and duties as the Arabo-Muslim Algerians, "they [the French Algerians] will blend with many different religions and customs."[27] But Camus's philosophy denies that there is a unity in all beings and things, according to his statement in Algiers:[28] "I believe only in differences, not in uniformity." The future would prove him right on this particular point, which Sénac had refuted.

Sénac meets Camus only once, on February 21, 1956, after the writer's return to Paris on January 25. Their political differences, hidden for a long time, are now out in the open—among their circle of friends—following the publication of Sénac's article in *Esprit* (March 1956).

Following his disappointing appeal in Algiers and the late discovery that he had been "trapped" by "Arab" friends who were part of the FLN, Camus—refusing to back down on France's presence in Algeria—begins his long and famous silence. An eloquent silence . . . one could add. What else could he say? His stance on a French Algeria would hardly evolve, between the spoken and the unspoken, as we will see. In this month of February 1956 the writer ceases his collaboration with *L'Express*[29]—which had become politically useless to him—just when Sénac began there as a literary chronicler, thanks to Claude Krief—his friend from Oran—who was the magazine's political editor since 1955.

From now on the two men avoided each other, and kept their distance even though they weren't yet separated. Moreover, their schedules and their travels (literary for Camus and militant for Sénac) made it impossible for them to meet. Nothing could bring about a reconciliation, not the four poems that Sénac dedicated to Camus—combined under the title "Les attentes [The expectations]," published in *Les Cahiers du Sud*[30] in April 1956 —not the latest book Camus sent to Sénac in May 1956,[31] *The Fall*—a title that corresponded perfectly to the state of their friendship—not even the temporary arrest in

Algiers of their longtime friend Jean de Maisonseul on the 26th of May. Their reactions to Maisonseul's indictment were actually diametrically opposite—on the one hand, Camus's interventions, which became part of literary history;[32] on the other hand, the poet's enthusiastic response concerning the fate of his friend who "saved the honor" of the French liberals.[33]

■   ■   ■

In Paris, in June 1956, Sénac begins to work on his major "combat" writings: *Le Soleil sous les armes*,[34] a manifesto, and *Diwân de l'État-Major* [Diwan of the General Staff],[35] a collection of poems. Sénac's new militant and contextual concept of literature doesn't keep him from mentioning, in a separate study, the "secessionist" spirit of the Algerianist writers, as well as Albert Camus and his friends "arbitrarily grouped in a School of Algiers."[36] He viewed the latter as true forerunners of a national Algerian literature as they became committed "in a climate of insecurity and of questioning that the previous generations hadn't experienced."[37]

Still, Camus's term "cutthroat" and his timid silence gnaw at Sénac's heart, and yet the poet remains faithful. In a rough draft written during that time, he's able to translate his political and emotional dilemma:

To Camus. Maybe it's masochism, but each time that I say something against you, I'm striking myself with a knife.

While the "son" dwells upon his anger, he can't emancipate himself from the authority of the "father," yet he becomes increasingly distant, knowing that he's right. A Christian martyr, Sénac prefers the sorrow of self-degradation to a mutiny that appears imminent. This state of mind, an "insomnia" in Camus's own words,[38] brings him to tears daily, according to Jacques Miel,[39] who became Sénac's de facto adopted son shortly after their meeting in Paris on August 17, 1956.

From September 1st to the 15th, the poet composes a poem titled "To Albert Camus, who called me a cutthroat."[40] In this revealing poem, Sénac assesses (provisionally) his overall experience with Camus, nicknamed "The Master of the Absolute." Sénac taunts his friend, whom he still loves, in an interior dialogue that constantly associates politics and love—a poetic art that was burgeoning within him. He criticizes Camus's inaction:

> The blood flows between you and other men / said the Poet / and you can no longer see . . .

and affirms his commitment to the struggle:

> Me, I will thrust my hands into the wounds / in order to stop the bleeding . . .

Sénac simultaneously develops his revolutionary conviction—imbued with religious references (he constantly justifies his position based on his religious faith)—in front of this "Master of the Absolute," who

> kept his hands clean (his icebergs!) / while the Poet frenetically wrote / and the Poet loved him.

The text includes expressions such as "Total Body," "the strait of Jabbok," "wound at the hip" that one finds ten years later—starting in September 1966—when love and revolution will be mixed with eroticism in the writing of *Avant-Corps* [Forebody].[41] It therefore provides important elements in the slow birth and the somewhat complex process of Jean Sénac's poetic inspiration. The only missing element is irony—a feature and a theme shared by both Sénac and Camus[42]—introduced as a punctuation mark in the poet's letters, poems, and prose starting in 1945. He goes as far as naming a "School of the Irony Mark"[43] on April 1, 1962.

We don't know if Sénac gave a copy of this poem to Camus. However, one text did trigger the admonition, even the anger of the "father." This was "Salut aux écrivains et artistes noirs [Salute to the black artists and writers]," written by the poet, signed by Kateb Yacine and Henri Kréa, and published in *Présence Africaine.*[44] In this anecdotal poem—addressed to the First Congress of Black Artists and Writers, which was held in Paris during September 19–22, 1956— Sénac reflects on the role of the poet, as everyone's voice, against the suffering of the Algerian people in their fight against colonialism. Camus considered it "unacceptable, indecent and despicable," according to Sénac.[45] This degree of severity seems both disproportionate and incomprehensible, especially since the poet wasn't speaking specifically against France or against his own community. Nevertheless, it further widened the gap between the two friends, Sénac seeing the writer less and less despite his many attempts. In addition, Camus was very busy (personal issues, the staging of William Faulkner's *Requiem for a Nun*, and the revision of his essay *Exile and the Kingdom*).

In the fall of 1956 the two friends grow further apart, without yet severing ties completely. In Algeria, "pacification" becomes an all-out war. Sénac is therefore increasingly in rebellion against the father's silence, especially given his generosity in other issues. Camus takes a public stance during the events in Hungary, on November 10, 1956, and after.[46] On the other hand, he was silent when five principal leaders of the FLN, traveling from Rabat to Tunis, were arrested by French authorities (October 22, 1956) after their plane was hijacked and flown to Algiers; and more significantly, he was silent after the failed French, English, and Israeli intervention in Egypt on November 5 and 6, which had given hope to the Algerian people and to Sénac during the Suez political crisis. Enraged, the poet finally wonders if Camus's "solidarity is[n't just] European," since Europe appears so often in his writings ("Notebooks," 1956).

His suspicion was warranted. Given that Camus came from a deplorably racist colonial environment—one that Sénac had denounced—was he prejudiced against the "Arabs"? While the question of a "racist Camus" has been raised elsewhere,[47] the writer—who always valued difference (as mentioned before)—perhaps admitted it himself when he told his teacher, Jean Grenier, that he couldn't live in Algeria "because of the Arabs."[48] Still, Camus is lucid—as demonstrated in his posthumous novel, *The First Man*—and is aware of the tacit racism between communities, each group being taught to see the other as infidel, for example. Under these conditions, how could he "unite the differences,"[49] as he had claimed? There is a real gap between public discourse and personal conviction.

Sénac couldn't wait any longer. After a failed attempt to meet with Camus, he writes him a long letter on November 15, 1956, which he fails to send (another trait of the poet: writing letters, some of them imaginary, to people that he didn't always know, and not mailing them for reasons related to his changing personality). In his draft, in the margin of the first page, he writes: "Not sent due to the categorical intervention of Kateb Yacine, who thinks that 'Camus must be spared for the time being, for political reasons.'"[50] In his letter, Sénac notes: "We respected your silence and tried to quiet within us the questions that it raised." He asks that he condemn the tortures and the massacres of the French army in Algeria—which the writer had denounced in 1947, regarding Madagascar[51]—adding, "If Scipion still speaks to you with such violence, it's because he refuses to join Chaerea." The allusion to *Caligula* is crucial and translates Sénac's state of mind in these dark times. Even though he's outraged, the "son" still refuses to break up with the "father":

> I'm not with him, Chaerea, but I can't be against him. A same flame burns our hearts.

The friendship withstands their political differences. Sénac quotes this passage abundantly (again not respecting the original, given the poet's habit of misappropriating citations)[52] in order to explain the extent of his disagreement with Camus—who "taught [him] to demand everything"[53] as the "resolute Scipion"[54] might have said.

The disagreement between Sénac and Camus is certainly real by the end of 1956, but it wasn't over yet. Their statements in 1957 show that it deteriorated rapidly.

CHAPTER 7

From a Literature of Combat to the Nobel Prize

The year 1957 marks a decisive turning point in the rupture between Sénac and Camus, a terrible rupture due to the complex nature of their friendship.

In January, Sénac publishes—in a little leftist cultural review, *Exigence*[1]—a text flamboyantly titled *Le Soleil sous les armes* [*The Sun under the Weapons*], and subtitled *Éléments d'une poésie de la résistance algérienne* [Poetics of the Algerian Resistance]. It was preceded with a strongly activist statement, "Contre la pacification de la poésie [Against the pacification of poetry]," (written no doubt by the review's editorial board). The issue also contains Franz Fanon's "Letter of resignation" to the residing minister Lacoste,[2] which he personally handed to Sénac in Paris on September 24, 1956, just before joining the FLN in Tunis (the author of *Black Skins, White Masks* had recently participated in the First Congress of Black Artists and Writers). Due to the violence of these two decidedly anti-French writings, the issue was confiscated upon its publication, causing it to disappear immediately.

Le Soleil sous les armes, started in July 1956 but curiously dated December 1956, is a poetic manifesto that speaks for an Algerian nation both wounded and ennobled by a long tradition of resistance against French colonialism. It contains most importantly the following jab at Camus:

> He who writes will never live up to those who die, Camus once said at a time when he hadn't yet repudiated the injustice of *The Just*.[3]

This citation, which Sénac commented on briefly, would have serious consequences. Aside from the pain it caused Camus—who received a copy of the review from the poet (and not anonymously as Olivier Todd states)[4]—it strengthened his resolution to never mention the Algerian tragedy: "I have decided to remain silent with respect to Algeria, so that I don't further contribute to its misfortune or to the idiocies that are being written."[5] This statement, which remained a handwritten note, became either the draft for a brief letter to Sénac, according to Roger Quilliot, or the draft for a letter that was never sent, according to Herbert Lottman. Or it was turned into a long letter dated February 10, 1957, according to Olivier Todd and Jacqueline Lévi-Valensi,[6] who nevertheless don't mention whether it was sent (an improbable hypothesis since Sénac never mentioned it). This brings us back to the debate that occurred privately between the two friends immediately after the beginning of the Algerian War.

Given the bare facts of reality, the debate on the "injustice of the *Just*" was no longer just academic for Sénac, but deeply political in nature. While in 1948 he had the soul of a pacifist ("I refuse, with Camus, any reason that justifies murder, whether good or bad"),[7] this changed in 1957, when he saw *The Just* as "politically . . . a critique of revolutionary violence."[8] Yet Camus couldn't accept that violence, and felt only "contempt for the killer of women and children." Therefore he refutes neither *The Just*, nor its philosophical version *The Rebel*, as stated in the draft of a letter to Sénac. Without having to theorize on the art of warfare, there never was, unfortunately, a "clean" or "surgical" war, as one would say today, which Camus could not accept at the time—apparently—due to his "political infantilism."[9] The Algerian War led to innocent deaths on both sides, yet the casuistic writer always seemed—in private—mostly concerned with his own people, whereas in his public speeches (in *Civil Truce*, and later in *Actuelles III* [*Algerian Chronicles*]) he condemns the murderers of civilians in both communities. Still, he speaks out only against the violence committed in the name of nationalism ("The cause of the Arabs in Algeria has never been more undermined by the civil terrorism now systematically carried out by the Arab movements"), and completely overlooks the practices of the French army. Camus ends the draft of his letter to Sénac with this admonition: "I would add that your 'not yet' isn't just incorrect, it's slightly insulting to a man who you know was the only one of his type, in Algeria, to defend the Arab people twenty years ago."

The writer had indeed condemned the perverted aspects of the colonial system, but did not question it as fundamentally as Sénac did.

Camus expressed his disagreement with Sénac in strong terms, and precipitated their breach. For the first time since the beginning of their friendship ten years earlier, Sénac didn't receive Camus's new book *Exile and the Kingdom*, published in March 1957.

One also notices that Camus's name doesn't appear in Sénac's notebooks, writings, or correspondence until his letter on September 18, 1957, cited by Todd[10] (we shall return to this), where he informs his friend that his request to fight in the Algerian *maquis* was denied "three times" by the political leaders of the FLN, who thought that his presence in France was more important.[11] Indeed, Sénac was continuously planning his return to war-torn Algeria "to discuss and to love, even at the cost of my life" (*Carnet 1955*, September 19). Nevertheless, for the reasons mentioned above and because of his poor finances, he never made it, contrary to Camus, who traveled there four times (February 17–March 1, 1955; January 18–25, 1956; March 26–April 12, 1958; April 20–29, 1959).

However, Sénac made a short trip to Italy with Jacques Miel, in particular to Florence and its surrounding area, during September 26–October 4, 1957. There he most certainly thought of Camus, who had praised the city in *Noces*, and had visited it three years earlier. He sent him a postcard dated September 26, according to O. Todd:

> Despite the falling out, despite the crimes of the Masters of the Vine, the terrible anger of my brothers, despite the night of blood that has engulfed us, I know that someday, together, we will find again the fraternal peace of Fiesole, the peace that I loved before finding it in the pages of *Nuptials*.[12]

These words place us once again at the heart of the passion between Sénac and Camus. The former remembers the "falling-outs," i.e., a chronological succession of crises between the two. Cyclical crises brought about by the "son's" irascible behavior toward his beloved "father," who taught him how to be happy in *Nuptials*, but who remains silent or still regarding the oppression of his "Arab" brothers by the "Masters of the Vine." (The "Masters of the Vine" meant, in the poet's language at the time, the declining "colonizers," i.e., the withering branches or vines of the vineyard—a quintessential symbol of colonial Algeria.)

The complicated sentimental alchemy between the two men (more emotional than cerebral in nature) persists. Sénac is split between literary concurrence and political antinomy when it came to the destiny of their homeland—in other words, between happiness and duty. He still keeps a "passionate" affection for Camus. Having heard from Suzanne Agnely how much his friend had been "hurt, outraged"[13] by his statement in *Exigence*, he removes the second part of the derogatory sentence ("at a time when he hadn't yet repudiated the injustice of the *Just*") for a newly edited and enriched version published in book form on October 1, 1957.

Le Soleil sous les armes was published by a small press in Rodez (Aveyron), directed by Jean Subervie (whom Sénac met in Paris on November 14, 1956), in spite of meager resources and "despite the risks of censorship."[14] Unlike the *Poèmes* collection, the book received mixed reviews. On January 7, 1958, the poet writes—in *L'Action* (based in Tunis), where he had been collaborating since January 1957[15]—"It's the conspiracy of silence, this book disturbs." Only a few professional critics—and of renown!—review it in France, such as Claude Roy, who identifies it as "one of the most important essays in recent times,"[16] and René Lacôte, who compares it to *L'Honneur des poètes*, published clandestinely in occupied France in 1943.[17] Most importantly, the work distances Sénac from the large publishers and from the Parisian editorial circles. Having been notified on August 26, Gallimard swiftly agrees that he publish the "text with another publisher,"[18] and disappoints him by rejecting both his poetry collections: *Diwân de l'État-Major* and *Désordres*. The first was more politically oriented, while the second was more personally inspired.

In a letter dated October 27, 1957,[19] Gallimard specifies in fact that in the first manuscript "the influence of Char and the desire to rewrite *Feuillets d'Hypnos* [Leaves of Hypnos] are only too apparent," while the second "hasn't removed the defects—i.e., a few "weaknesses"—noted in the first version of the work." However, in Sénac's *Journal* dated December 23, 1955, it is stated that Gallimard had "unanimously" agreed to publish *Les Désordres* (with a few minor reservations) and that one just needed to "wait," as Camus had said. Also, Sénac disregards the reasons given by the publisher and sees in this refusal "a formal veto from Camus," as he wrote to Robert Llorens on March 5, 1958.[20] This doesn't prevent him from sending a copy of *Soleil sous les armes* to the writer on November 7, a few days after the Nobel Prize for Literature is awarded on October 17. Their friendship seems to be on the mend since the poet receives a picture of Camus printed for the occasion (with the banner "Albert Camus, Nobel Prize for Literature 1957"), with the following autograph:

For Jean Sénac, in anticipation of a reconversion that would finally serve the glory of our homeland. Hoping that we will join the glorious pack of his friends with open eyes. His A. C.[21]

Like Jean-Pierre Péroncel-Hugoz,[22] one wonders what the term "homeland [*patrie*]" encompassed in Camus's thinking. Is it the Algerian Algeria that Sénac defended, or the French Algeria that Camus envisioned, although reshaped politically? For the poet—who considered himself first as "Algerian" in 1950, then as Algerian who loved France "my second homeland" starting in 1952[23]—a homeland "is forged and earned"[24] in the struggle against the occupying masters, castigated for being neither part of its "race" nor of its "people." As for Camus, for whom Spain was a second homeland,[25] what was then the first? There are too many clues in his own writings[26] and in those of his commentators—some of which distinguish wisely between homeland (France) and country (Algeria)[27]—to be developed here. We will limit ourselves to the writer's own concept at the time of the Algerian War.

Solitary despite his international fame, Camus nevertheless remains committed to the French Algerians, as reported by the journalist Jean Daniel:

If the violence continues, one's duty, even for someone like myself, will be to return to one's community since it would be impossible to remain neutral or external.[28]

Ever since the failed call for a civil truce, war was ubiquitous in Algeria, and Robert Lacoste's "last five minutes" (declaration on November 20, 1956) further reduced the prospect of a resolution and of peace. In addition to the "Battle of Algiers" (January–September 1957), there are daily bombings, arrests, death sentences, disappearances, attacks, executions, massacres, and tortures. The persistence of violence divides the metropolitan French and gives the conflict an international dimension. The time for compromise is over, and Camus's options become increasingly clear: in an Algeria comprised of two peoples, "those who are Muslim and those [who] aren't,"[29] he undeniably chooses his "own kind," "his family"—"their unhappiness is my own, we are of the same blood,"[30] he wrote five years earlier in "Retour à Tipasa," an essay edited by Sénac for the review *Terrasses* as mentioned earlier. Within the existing power dynamics, this literary idea betrays its true political nature. Whereas the poet had long since crossed the border between the two communities of Algeria, to the point of no return, Camus seems to disregard it in his autograph, where he hopes for his friend's "conversion." Does he intentionally hide his obvious differences with Sénac, which the latter expressed on many occasions during their conversations as well as in his writings?

Camus's writings in this context are not those of a "torn" man (the famous dilemma between yes and no), as his friends and critics had so often observed, but of a partisan of French Algeria, whose concerns about its loss were both justified and legitimate. His other observations fully confirm this. Upon receiving ethnologist Germaine Tillion, on October 1, 1957, he "despairs about the future."[31] This despair increases upon Charles de Gaulle's return to power (he met with him on March 5, 1958, and spoke about "the risk of turmoil if Algeria is lost").[32] After the events of May 13, 1958, in Algiers (French *ultras*, protesting against the FLN's execution of three French soldiers, took over the headquarters of the General Government, and the army seized power by creating a pro-French Algerian "Committee of Public Safety"), and those on the eve of June 1, 1958 (inauguration of de Gaulle, the last president of the Fourth Republic's

Council, by the National Assembly), Camus responds with this explicit mandate, on May 29: "My job is to write books and to fight when the freedom of my close ones and of my people is threatened."[33] Unlike the majority of French Algerians who saw de Gaulle as the guardian of French Algeria, Camus—who was both distraught and lucid—laments every day: "my lost country" (July 25, 1958);[34] "if my land is lost, I will be useless" (July 29, 1958);[35] "it's perhaps too late for Algeria" (August 4, 1958).[36] All of these confessions, unpublished at the time but echoed in *Actuelles III: Chroniques algériennes* in June 1958,[37] converge implicitly with Camus's public declarations and clarifications after the Nobel Prize (its announcement and the award ceremony), which aggravated the tensions with Sénac. While the writer doesn't mention French Algeria directly, some of his statements imply it.

These statements, comprised of a group of four texts published in the Parisian press during the last trimester of 1957—in the weekly magazine *Demain*, the monthly journal *La Revue prolétarienne* (subtitled *Revue syndicaliste révolutionaire*), and the daily newspaper *Le Monde*[38]—are fairly explicit and represent his position clearly. They are contradicted by Sénac (and by reality itself), who, the day after Camus's declaration at the University of Stockholm on December 12, 1957, responds virulently in "Camus to Lacoste's rescue?"[39]

Written in the form of a question that was meant to fulfill a polemical objective and to reinforce Sénac's obvious political stance, this article from December 18, 1957, establishes in fact their differences once and for all. He believes he's been sufficiently respectful of the silence of his friend, who now "serves dubious politics" not expressed publicly, but obviously close to those who defend French Algeria. Sénac is nevertheless unable to publicly abandon a teacher to whom he owes "too much," and decides to cancel the publication of his text. He communicates this to Camus[40] and answers with "affectionate anger,"[41] on December 21, 1957. Sénac prefers avoiding the "noisy public confusion," in order "to stay away from a particular group of barkers . . . for whom Algeria is but a pretext for parading,"[42] as mentioned in a letter to Robert Llorens. This unwillingness to take part in a political debate, which is essentially public, suggests that the poet chooses to maintain—away from everyone—his personal dialogue with the beloved "father," despite the anger caused by his political views.

In fact, the reasons that Sénac invokes in his correspondence with Llorens are different than what he expresses in a letter to Camus on December 18, 1957, where the poet states that he was "relieved" to cancel the publication of his article—which he describes as "parricide"—after reading the correction published by the winner of the Nobel Prize in *Le Monde*. He adds: "This doesn't essentially change anything in our particular positions, nor the certainty that I know some of the deeper reasons for your silence." Emphasizing that he is not part of the FLN, Sénac adds: "If I'm not in the mountains, in the *Maquis*, it's because they rejected me three times." He legitimizes his position—being both independent (which doesn't keep him from being "loyal to both the oppressed Arabs and the blinded Europeans") and obedient to Camus's philosophy (that of *The Just*, since he's willing to give up his own life for someone else's)—with references that are strongly Christian, and even Christ-like: "I try to serve love and not hatred, at the very heart of violence"; "the word becomes flesh and lives among us"; "my victory is not of this world."

As mentioned before, Sénac's religious faith can largely explain, if not justify, his political activism. He concludes: "In my first letter to you, 11 years ago, I wrote that I was a Christian anarchist. Today that statement makes me smile. But there's a baptism there, a spiritual order to which I remain loyal, especially since I have a better understanding of what that tiny word "Algerian" means, and the commitment that it demands from us." Christianity as he sees it, even though it might seem heretical, requires that he participate in political struggles. He keeps reminding Camus of this, a secular Camus, whose philosophy and commitment are driven by humanist principles without any religious connotations.

As for Camus's answer, the "affectionate anger" that Sénac mentioned was certainly real. The Nobel laureate notes that "this nice prosecution" is built "on hearsay, unfathomable for anyone who knows me a little, and before I was even able to correct myself." Disappointed by the poet's attitude, he reminds Sénac of the many contributions he made, for him and for Algeria: "I wasn't lucky enough to preserve in you the simple memory, concerning you and concerning the Algerian people." While this was the first time Camus used that expression to designate the majority of Algerians, he still returns to his "casuistry of blood" when addressing to the poet "this last advice," a somewhat desperate one:

If you continue to speak of love and fraternity, do not write any more poems glorifying the bomb that indiscriminately kills the child and the dreadful "blind" adult. That poem, which continues to weigh heavily on my heart, took away any value to your arguments, so little assured I am of the value of my own. Good luck.

This letter is, to our knowledge, the last one that Camus wrote to Sénac, and its tone and content herald the inevitable.

Sénac makes no mistake about it in his response, on December 24, 1957, to his "impossible" friend (an impossible friendship, like one would say an "impossible love," he writes), and this "before we become engulfed once again in the thick silence of our small convulsive prides." The poet in turn corrects each item of Camus's letter, while expanding the various ideas expressed in his article. Thus, regarding the poem "written in honor of the bomb" he states that he will not rescind it since it wasn't an elegy but a "simple [and] unequivocal recognition" of a reality. Even though he sometimes "kills with the Word," he's surprised that Camus didn't grasp his other poem in honor of "Captain Alexander" (René Char's nickname during the Resistance), where he repeated some of the poet's lines (taken from *Leaves of Hypnos*) praising violence. On the very issue of violence, he sees its arbitrariness on both sides:

I cannot condemn the Revolution, any more than I can my friend from Bab-El-Oued who lynches and massacres an "Arab" following the explosion at the Casino de la Corniche [on June 9, 1957]. They're in the grip of a "human" passion that can no longer worry about morals (which we haven't bothered to teach them anyway).

This tragedy was a consequence of colonialism, Sénac adds. He mentions again that he supports the FLN and those who fight for Algeria—whose independence is "inevitable." This support enabled him to "reconsider the meaning of [his] solidarity with [his] community and the meaning of [his] attachment to France." Concerning Camus's particular position on this issue, the poet points out that the writer hasn't changed since his articles in *Alger Républicain*:

I always notice the tragic back and forth, the contradictions, the misunderstanding, the ambiguity of words that are simultaneously those of an honest man and those of an unforgivable "con-man"[43] ["louette" in Pied-noir] whose register is too vague to produce any melody.

Finally, concerning the duty of memory, Sénac writes that he has always upheld it, ever since he followed Léon Bloy's own precept: "An obedient son of the Church, I'm nevertheless in eager communion with all those who are outraged, disappointed, deceived, all the damned of this world."

In order to appreciate the polemical implications of Camus's four pieces, one can highlight the following "contradictions," which Sénac was going "to blow wide open" in his article "Camus to the rescue of Lacoste?"

In *Demain*, Camus states:

We have built, by virtue of a generous dialogue and true solidarity, a community of Algerian writers, French and Arab. This community is split in two, momentarily. But men like Feraoun, Mammeri, Chraïbi, Dib, and so many others, have taken their place among European writers.

Sénac cites these passages (and others) and contests them furiously. According to him there was neither dialogue nor solidarity between writers of both communities, except—he points out—among a few writers of French origin (Henri Kréa, Jean-Pierre Millecam) who, with their Arabo-Berber peers, had sided to various degrees with "the Algerian people's struggle for liberation."

Here the poet was somewhat excessive in this response. An inclusive dialogue, even if modest or marginal, had truly existed in Algeria between writers of its various communities. During the interwar period we can mention *Les Compagnons du jardin* [The companions of the garden] (1933), a book jointly written by Abdelkader Fikri and Robert Randau,[44] which deals with the issues facing Algeria in the '30s during the centenary celebration of French conquest. We should also mention that after the Second World War, aside from the Sidi Madani meetings (January–March 1948), literary reviews such as *Forge* (1946–1947) and those directed by Sénac himself—*Soleil* (1950–1952) and *Terrasses* (1953)—not counting the publishers (like Charlot, Baconnier), had warmly welcomed non-indigenous native writers—and this without any "colonialist" or "paternalistic" intention, as Sénac improperly believed—solely for the "quality" and the originality of their writings.

As for the idea that the aforementioned writers cited by Camus had taken their place among their "European" colleagues, instead of the cultural sphere where they had been—traditionally—segregated, Sénac replies: "One could think he never read them!"

The issue of national identity for Algerian writers has been problematic ever since, and has generated heated debates beyond the country's independence. Prior to the Algerian War, these writers weren't perceived as "Algerian" or "French," even less as "Europeans," among the rare critics that were interested in their works. Neither *jus soli* (right of the land), nor *jus sanguinis* (right of the blood)—the two main criteria for the legal recognition of nationality under French law—had given them a "literary nationality," to cite Malek Haddad's famous expression.[45] While they used the language of the Other [French], they were differentiated from the other "Algerian" writers, i.e., the French that were native or non-native of Algeria. They were identified—even by Camus— through the heavily ideological and reductive frameworks of race ("Arabs") and religion ("Muslims"). If critics sometimes related them to the *École d'Alger*, their literature stands in complete contrast to the literary movement, which refuses any form of political activism. In addition to a literature that witnesses a dominated society from the inside, this generation (called that of "1952," composed mainly of the three novelists mentioned by Camus) provides, with the outbreak of the Algerian War, another literature for another Algeria.

These writers, joined by a few others of European descent such as Sénac, appropriated the term "Algerian" in order to define themselves. Sénac, who was the first to formulate a definition of postcolonial Algerian literature that broke away from Algerianism and the *École d'Alger*, stated that "Any writer who had definitely sided with the Algerian nation is an Algerian writer."[46] Since 1953 (the same year *Terrasses* was launched), he fought for a "National Front of Algerian thought"[47] and was glad to see Féraoun, Dib, and Kateb join him on this specific issue: that the Algerian writer be a "lucid witness" among "the nation's first and foremost pioneers."[48] Such a concept is obviously different from that of Camus, who was opposed to any regional Algerian literature. In his eyes—according to Sénac—Algerian literature goes back to the African Latinism defended by Louis Bertrand. Was Saint Augustine, that "wog" according to François Mauriac, not part of his specialized degree in philosophy? As for the Islamic period, Camus disregards it and reduces it to "cities without a past," or even "dark centuries" (term used by the pro-colonialist historian Émile-Félix Gautier). Camus would nevertheless be recognized as "Algerian" by [Mouloud] Feraoun and a few others, in the famous issue of *Simoun* that Sénac boycotts on June 1, 1960.[49]

Sénac is "embarrassed"[50] by the term even though ten years earlier he wrote, in one of his first literary articles, that Camus was "of authentically Algerian parents—with all that it implies in terms of hybridity and people"[51]—and that his books "derived their substance from the Algerian soil."[52] The identification of Camus with "being Algerian" was obviously literary since, aside from "The Guest" (in *Exile and the Kingdom*),[53] he had only defended a political Algeria in his journalism.

In *La Révolution prolétarienne* [The proletarian revolution], according to Sénac, Camus "takes a public and violent stance against the 'crimes' of the FLN, disregarding systematically those committed by the opposing movement, the MNA, and by [France's] pacification." Such an attitude reveals ideological views that can easily be tied to those of the various governments under the Fourth Republic. Like the Nobel laureate, they deliberately conflate the issue to the point of denying—even semantically—any nationalist intention to "the insurrection" or "the rebellion" seen as a "war of liberation" or "revolution" among the protagonists or sympathizers (including Sénac) and as a "conflict of decolonization" among international public opinion.

In addition, they [the governments under the Fourth Republic] simultaneously encourage an internal Algerian War between the FLN and the MNA—on both fronts (in Algeria and in France, through immigration)—and the acceleration of "pacification" both militarily (expansion of war operations) and socially (implementation of specialized administrative Sections, the famous SAS, structures that maintained the colonial presence in rural areas under the supervision of military officers that were often Islamophiles).

Consequently, Sénac is correct in saying that Camus's political position, i.e., his unilateral silence, is "that of *raison d'état*, or if you will, reason of civilization." He still can't accept that his friend cultivates false interpretations of "revolutionary terrorism" while expressing his solidarity with the European victims of totalitarianism (Nazism, Francoism, Communism) and remaining silent on the French army's massacres in Algeria, since whether "French or Arab, it's the blood of men that is being spilled."[54] For Sénac, Camus's Eurocentrism endorses a French thought with strong "imperialist and conservative" leanings. It's a "right-wing discourse from a leftist man."[55]

Moreover, the "son"—who was constantly relating Camus's work to Algerian politics—can't accept that his playwright "father" dedicates passages "to Kaliayev's admirable remorse," but refuses to bear witness to those of Ben Sadok and Taleb, both pure characters from *The Just* in their own ways, i.e., authentic revolutionaries like Stepan, the anti-Camus (Taleb is Ahmed Taleb-Ibrahimi, while Ben Sadok is Mohamed Ben Sadok or Saddok, an FLN militant who gunned down Ali Chekkal, previous vice-president of the Algerian Assembly, at the Colombes stadium in Paris on May 26, 1957. Jean-Paul Sartre and André Mandouze testified during the trials in December 1957, and Camus intervened by writing a letter to the president of the Criminal Court).[56] Camus is aware, though, in 1957–1958, that his play is timely.[57] Was his purpose, given his sympathy for the Russian nihilists of 1905, to transpose their story to the Algerian tragedy? In light of his political convictions, "the Arabs" perhaps weren't worthy of becoming "The Just."

For Sénac, Camus was going against his own morals in his disregard for the Algerian struggle. He had always called for a greater "justice," even "reparation," for the Arabs, and yet he never clearly defined those terms, which remained abstract, pure rhetoric without substance. As a product of colonialism he couldn't be free from it, especially when on both sides of the Mediterranean "people" (public opinion, intellectuals, friends, or rivals) were demanding that he be the conscience of Algeria. Yet, the writer continuously thought as a Frenchman, and one can't force a man to relinquish his origins, or to stop thinking "French," as Sénac wrote. Camus's concept of justice was very much connected, as in the following statement: "I have chosen justice in order to remain, on the contrary, faithful to the land."[58] His political foes nevertheless see him as a "just man without justice," as Simone de Beauvoir famously said.[59]

Finally, Camus's statements to the students at the University of Stockholm on December 12, 1957—published by *Le Monde* on December 14—irritate Sénac greatly, making the friendship still "more difficult" according to Roger Quilliot.[60]

Sénac responds ironically to his friend's untruthful statement regarding the "total and reassuring freedom of metropolitan press," which strangely coincided with a confiscation at *France Observateur*, for the third time. Camus seems to ignore (or maybe pretends to ignore) the significant restrictions on the freedom of the press (and of publishing in general), enforced by the law of April 3rd declaring the "state of emergency" in Algeria, and further reinforced by that of March 10, 1956, instituting "special powers." Camus quickly corrects himself in a letter to *Le Monde* on December 17, 1957, in which he firmly disapproves of the restrictions on the freedom of the press while maintaining that they were "relatively small"[61] with respect to the Algerian War. The historian Benjamin Stora,[62] on the other hand, writes that "under the Fourth Republic certain newspapers were particularly targeted," notably the "four giants of French counter-propaganda" (Jacques Soustelle), *France Observateur*, as mentioned, as well as *L'Express*, *Le Monde*, and *Témoignage chrétien*. Reacting with patriotic impulse, Camus adopts a point of view close to that of the various governments "bogged down in the Algerian tragedy."[63]

During these times of war, censorship wasn't affecting only metropolitan France. Neither Camus nor Sénac mentioned the censorship that Algerians— both in France and in Algeria—were subjected to. "Nowhere did the colonial power weigh more, and for a longer period of time, than on the Algerian writers and artists," Laurent Goblot remarks in his pamphlet *Apologie de la censure: Petite histoire de la censure à travers les ages et les régimes* [Apology of censorship: A little history of censorship through the ages and regimes].[64] Without providing names or figures, this statement relates to what Sénac wrote in *Le Soleil sous les armes*, on a situation that paradoxically preceded the Algerian War, and which even affected Camus.

In his brief comment regarding the "relatively small mistakes" made by several French governments when dealing with the Algerian problem, Sénac doesn't mention (perhaps did he forget?) Camus's correction in *Le Monde*. The Nobel laureate states, in fact, that the "mistakes" regarded only the freedom of the press. In many ways it seems inconceivable that Camus's statement was meant to describe the entire Algerian situation. Sénac's outrage, even though it was understandable (those "relatively small mistakes," he writes, were the cause of "thousands of Arab and French deaths"), has little to do with Camus's actual statement. In his defense of a partisan cause, the poet tends toward spurious exaggerations even though his good faith is unquestionable on this very issue.

Sénac also comments on Camus's concept (which the writer didn't mention in his statement, if one looks at his press release) of a "personal federalism (and not territorial) in which all of Algeria's French, Berber and Arab communities would be equally represented by an Assembly." Aside from the fact that this concept was, in the eyes of the poet, only a "more liberal arrangement of Algeria as an integral part of France"—promoted by every French government—he couldn't imagine how one could establish, legally and practically, an institutional system that in itself would represent an evolving sociopolitical reality in constant and conflicting evolution. Camus's proposal for an Algerian solution (political solution from a man who had, for many years, refused to take part in Algerian politics) was an understatement as usual. He didn't explain what his project would actually entail (looking remarkably like the General Statute for Algeria, ratified on September 20, 1947, which failed, to the writer's own acknowledgment); nor does he explain how to implement it constitutionally (he did so a few months later, in *Actuelles III*, in a pragmatic analysis of his own theory).

For Sénac, more of a realist than his friend, who was acting here as a political philosopher (although his contributions were unoriginal and mostly based on the theories of Vincent Lauriol, law professor at the University of Algiers), such a concept was, more than a "utopia, a criminal fraud that would be costly" in terms of human lives, and would delay a solution. The poet's answer was to negotiate towards the independence of Algeria, whereas Camus viewed independence as "a manifestation of the new Arab imperialism, which Egypt—assuming its own power—was hoping to lead."[65] Sénac would be proven correct against Camus, who was increasingly Eurocentric with regard to Algeria.

Finally, Sénac returns to Camus's unilateral condemnation of terrorism (and indirectly, that of "rebellion"), which apparently concerned only his mother and his family. The poet would have "subscribed" to this "moving declaration" (according to his own words) had the writer stigmatized all violence, i.e., no matter who the perpetrator was, and no matter who the victim was—whether Arab or French—Camus having always shown compassion for the latter in public. Sénac denounces the imposture, particularly the famous statement that fell as a verdict: "I believe in justice, but I would defend my mother before justice."

This expression, subject to so much controversy and analysis, is still famous, notably among Algerians, who quote it either with suspicion[66] or condemnation[67] whenever Camus or his position on the Algerian War are mentioned. Sénac, obsessed with its strong political undertone, responded to Camus (in his letter on December 18, 1957: "I try to defend both my mother and justice"), and repeated the expression in his literary works (poetry, theater, various articles). In his play *Le Soleil interdit* [The forbidden sun] (an unpublished tragedy on the forbidden love between Jérôme and Malika—a French man and an Algerian woman—on the eve of the Algerian War), two of his characters say the following:

> If we order you to kill your mother for the sake of the people, would you do it? Without hesitating he answered, "yes," but once the reckless passion had passed: "no, I think that I would try to kill, in a frightful struggle, the principles in her that are wrong."

In an original draft, without a date but probably written in 1958–1959, Sénac had come to the following conclusion:

> Camus was my father. Having to choose between my father and justice, I chose justice.

Fifteen years later (in 1972) the poet, echoing the famous statement, conveyed the following to Jean-Pierre Péroncel-Hugoz: "I defended both my mother and justice since I was able to rally her to the side of justice."[68] This is incorrect since, according to the letters she wrote to her son, she was less than enthusiastic about Algeria's independence. In January 1973, Sénac in fact told us that Camus had made that statement, "in the heat of the moment, without really believing it." But for us he was an "Algerian" in his own way, according to an Arab tradition where one says, in reference to the sorrow of a vanquished enemy: "May his mother cry and not mine."

Thus, the split between Sénac and Camus seems irreversible at the end of 1957. The poet's resentment is at its peak, but the exact moment of the final separation of the father and the son is difficult to determine given the documentation we currently have. In light of the poet's writings, and the accounts of his close friends, we can only assume that it was sometime in 1958. Even though Sénac states that he had broken up with Camus "a long time ago,"[69] in a letter to Llorens on March 25, 1958, and confirms it again to the poet Djamel Amrani (whom he met in May 1958),[70] it's difficult to determine given that he continued writing to Camus. We can nevertheless try to outline the stages of a separation that was as turbulent as their friendship was passionate.

It seems that we can date the last meeting between Sénac and Camus to January–February 1958. We can refer to Lottman's book,[71] in which he mentions that, according to Suzanne Agnely, "a writer from Algeria arrived, a longtime friend; he showed up at Gallimard, and in an excited voice asked to see Camus." There followed a verbal altercation concerning the Nobel laureate's unwillingness to support Algeria's struggle. Lottman doesn't mention the writer's name, but dates the event—without much precision—sometime after Camus's Nobel Prize (the writer returns from Sweden on December 15, 1957) and before his next to last visit to Algeria in March/April 1958. There's reason to believe that it was Jean Sénac, since Jean de Maisonseul mentions a similar incident (which he heard from Suzanne Agnely in 1960 soon after Camus's death) occurring during the last meeting between Sénac—who couldn't be the "*ennemi* brother" any longer—and Camus, in his office at Gallimard. Jean de Maisonseul tells the following:

> All of a sudden, she heard yells coming from the office of Camus (which never happened), who kicked out Sénac for having called him a coward. We can imagine his Spanish indignation! After a long moment of silence, fearing that he was unwell, she finds him leaning over his desk, his head between his arms, tears in his eyes; he tells her: "And what if that kid was right." Suzanne Agnely didn't tell me when this occurred, only that it was right after the Nobel Prize.[72]

In an "Open letter to Jules Roy," included in his unfinished book project *Pieds-noirs, mes frères* [*Pieds-noirs*, my brothers] (March 1962), Sénac mentions that one day he had been "expelled" from the office of Camus, who considered him a "cutthroat."[73]

While Todd thought that Sénac was being "odious,"[74] the latter was perhaps recalling—as someone who had such a deep understanding of the work and political thought of his friend and teacher—Camus's axiom in "Vers un dialogue" [Toward a dialogue], an article whose title was so symptomatic of their friendship: "But I always thought," writes Camus in November 1946, "that the man who found hope in the human condition was 'crazy,' while the one who despaired from events was a coward."[75] And, as mentioned earlier, Camus was increasingly desperate concerning the future of Algeria, especially after the arrival of de Gaulle, when words as much as bullets were accelerating the loss of his land, i.e., the independence of Algeria, Sénac's objective dream. Was the latter, decidedly a careful reader of Camus, correct in his terrible remark even though the injury affected the victim as much as its author?

After that last meeting, the interactions between Sénac and Camus become even murkier. The ambiguity is further maintained by Sénac, who mentions Camus's name several times in his *Carnet 1958* (the last one, on November 12, indicated that the poet had given a typed copy of *Soleil interdit*—a play that he finished on November 9, 1958, in Paris—to Jacques Lemarchand and to Camus, at Gallimard). Sénac even speaks favorably of Camus at two public events, which further reveals his paradoxical personality, especially with regard to the Nobel laureate:

In Grenoble, at a conference he facilitated on March 4, 1958, titled "Le Poète algérien dans la cité [The Algerian poet in the city]," (organized under the auspices of L'Association des *Étudiants Musulmans Nord-Africains* [The Association of Muslim North African Students] and L'Union de la Gauche Socialiste [The Union of the Socialist Left]), Sénac—in an expanded reiteration of *Soleil sous les armes*—underlines Camus's political role as a young Algerian: "Like so many others Albert Camus, at a time when he was a militant for the Algerian Cause, came into conflict with the General Government."[76] He curiously relates this partisan struggle of the past with those of the present, his own and those of Kateb Yacine and of his friends, writers and artists M'Hamed Issiakhem, Abdellah Benanteur, and Louis Nallard.

In an interview for Radio Paris's literary program "Les Voix de l'avant-garde [The voices of the avant-garde],"[77] on May 15, 1958, the poet situates a number of North African writers with respect to French literature. Naming Camus and a few others (Jean Amrouche, Emmanuel Roblès, Jules Roy, and himself), he points out: "We were colonials," meaning that they were local authors who could write just as well as their "Parisian counterparts" or the "classical writers." This desire to prove themselves to the metropolitan French (who are simultaneously equal and different) is why, according to Sénac, novelists such as Camus strive for a "fervent classicism." The interview (as well as other writings in that same year, 1958)[78] clearly indicates that Sénac, despite his political militancy for a different Algeria, wanted to emphasize his French cultural origins.

In light of this, one wonders if Sénac had seen Camus again and spoken to him. The mystery remains, and is further reinforced by Jean de Maisonseul, who had seen the poet and the writer silently pass each other at the opening of his show in Paris, at the Lucie Weill gallery[79] on May 9, 1958. The painter wasn't aware of their dispute since neither of them had mentioned it.[80] The only thing we know for certain is that the poet's last letter to Camus was on April 29, 1958.

On that day, shaken up by the news that Taleb Abderrahmane, a student in chemistry, had been executed on April 24, 1958, after eleven months of detention and torture (he made bombs for the FLN), Sénac wrote an article in which he furiously denounced the "executioners of Algiers."[81] He sends it to Camus—whom he now calls "The Nobel laureate for the Defense of Europe and of French Algeria,"[82] and "Nobel laureate for Pacification"[83]—and chastises him: "Taleb was a modern brother to Kaliayev ... Couldn't you demand [his] pardon? Had you used your fame for that purpose only, you would have reclaimed it with renewed strength and a clear face." Always harsh and excessive in his treatment of Camus, Sénac was unaware that his friend had already defended Taleb Abderrahmane.[84] Also, was he aware that the writer had intervened multiple times in favor of many other Algerians condemned by the French authorities during the Algerian War, in order to have their death sentences lifted and to free them from prison?[85] Through these actions—for those who were putting him on "trial"—Camus redeemed himself and met his moral obligations. Having failed in political endeavors (civil truce, federalist project), he turned to concrete acts. And saving lives is more important than political contingency, which can be dramatic but short-lived.

Ultimately, the rupture between Sénac and Camus is partially a consequence of a misunderstanding. It was the result of a political and sentimental disagreement between two men who mutually disappointed each other, a mistake between a loving "son" and the loved "father." Upon the writer's death, on January 4, 1960, the poet ends his "parricide" by making—that same night—a final statement on their friendship in his unfinished "novel":

O Father, why open my eyes if it's only to show me Roman ruins and misunderstandings?[86]

This bitter question encapsulates the son's resentment towards his father, who still believed in an Algeria of the past (Latin and belonging of a certain France) and who remained ambivalent about its present. Camus's death "freed" him in the sense that he was untethered from the informal tutelage of that "terrible father." Yet, he couldn't deny what the writer had given him in his own life. This was—precisely—the point of view of Jules Roy, who quickly left for Algeria (in spring 1960) in order to investigate and returned with his piece: *La Guerre d'Algérie*.

The "son" nevertheless keeps the door open when he writes that Camus remains, despite everything, "a potential brother," and that he plans to dedicate "an entire book to [his] glory and [his] repudiation."[87] Sénac never wrote that book, but in another project, *Pieds-noirs, mes frères*, he incorporated (in March 1962) his last three letters to Camus with the writer's response. The work would have included all of his political thinking on Algeria, both published and unpublished, linked to the immediate political events as he explicitly suggested in the subtitle: *Contre le nihilisme de l'OAS/Le cri d'espoir d'un Algérien* [Against OAS nihilism/An Algerian's cry of hope].[88] Soon after he embarks on this project—quickly abandoned like so many others—upon his return from Marseille, Sénac stops by Lourmarin on April 16, 1962, in order to visit Camus's grave and photograph it.[89] That same day he notes in *Carnet 1962* the following comment that Francine Camus allegedly made about him (probably conveyed by a third party): "Yes, I knew him . . . I gave up hoping." The wife thus adopts her husband's attitude regarding any alteration in Sénac's political views. The poet was finally moved when he saw Camus's children waiting for a bus in the cold air of Lourmarin. As soon as he returns to Paris, he writes a series of articles revealing little-known aspects of Camus's work.

CHAPTER 8

Sénac, Reader of Camus

U pon Camus's death, Sénac didn't anticipate (as we saw in his writing on January 4, 1960) how much their friendship would survive and would find, in his own work, a singular posthumous destiny.

We mentioned a few of the thematic elements in Camus's work that Sénac presented in his journalistic articles and radio programs. In 1962 the poet decides to revisit them, by publishing two studies on the author's most famous work, "Notes sur *L'Etranger* d'Albert Camus" and "Notes complémentaires sur *L'Etranger* d'Albert Camus."[1] These texts, which weren't published until much later, provide both original and noteworthy insights, even to this day. In his "analysis" of *The Stranger*, Sénac offers both a political and literary reading— due to the Algerian War[2]—and his interpretations were later "confirmed" by Camus critics.

According to its author, *The Stranger* is a novel of "ambiguity,"[3] but Sénac tries to perceive it through the dualism, if not ambivalence, of a Janus-Camus both on the formal level and on the social-historical level.

On the formal plane, Sénac identifies themes in the novel that trace back to

Betwixt and Between and *Nuptials*, and continue in *Exile and the Kingdom*. From these three works, he sheds light on several aspects of Meursault, primarily the innocence of his character, i.e., his sincerity, his simplicity, and his refusal to lie. The sun and the sea are "actors," "protagonists," that bring their truth to the main character who evolves "halfway between misery and the sun," between beauty and humility, between the sensual celebration of the body and indifference to others.

Sénac locates the actual sites in Camus's novel that had been "reinvented," according to him, in particular the famous beach of the crime scene, which was a combination of two beaches of Algiers from the neighborhoods of Saint-Eugène and the Roman baths east of Algiers. All the other critics had opted for the one in Trouville (near Oran), based on Camus's *Carnets I*.[4]

Moreover, according to the poet, Meursault isn't just a symbol for European society. A real individual had significantly contributed to the creation of the literary character. Camus had stated that "Three people went into the composition of *The Stranger*: two men (including me) and a woman."[5] Unaware of that information (*Carnets II* weren't published until 1964, yet Sénac was very familiar with his friend's work as previously mentioned), the poet attributes to Meursault the features of Camus or his mother. Most importantly he points out that the main model is none other than Sauveur Galliéro, mentioned previously, and he reveals that "the whole beginning of *The Stranger* owes much to Galliéro, in particular the swim on the pier with Marie (Nicole) and the Fernandel movie the day after his mother's death. Sauveur was a perfect embodiment of that breed of young Gods that Camus spoke about; he enjoyed life naturally, without cheating."

Sénac is—to our knowledge—the first to have mentioned this detail, published for the first time in 1967. That same year—coinciding with the filming of Luchino Visconti's movie *The Stranger*—a retrospective show dedicated to Galliéro, and prefaced by Jean Sénac, was organized at the French Cultural Center of Algiers (May 25 to June 10). In the show's catalog Sénac wrote: "Based on one of his photos where we see him on the pier with Nicole, Marcello Mastroianni tried to recreate that "natural" look of *The Stranger*." Jean Cathelin, journalist at the *Nouvel Observateur* who had known Sénac since 1950, repeated almost word for word this information* that had gone unnoticed.[6]

On a sociohistorical level, Sénac sees in *The Stranger* a portrait of the colonizer, a political thesis that has often been explored since then. From that angle the poet notices—like any careful reader of Camus—the absence of Arabs,[7] "that absence which, for over a century, will shape human relations in Algeria," and that only a war could reveal.

Sénac sees that in all of Camus's works (narratives, lyrical essays, novellas) the Arabs are just "motionless, undefined, silent, unnamed forms." In the novel, Meursault manifests either complete indifference towards them, or a slight unease, out of fear that these anonymous shadows might leap out "with a knife." Hence his "normal" response, one of annoyance more than regret, when he kills the Arab. Sénac notices that "he doesn't have any more remorse than a cowboy who kills an Indian." The murderous sun, according to the poet, is manifested in Meursault's name, which is "mort" [death] and "soleil" [sun].

Sénac notices from that perspective that like Meursault, Camus—the writer and the man—"has the typical reactions, the mentality of his people." Contrary to the Muslim population, Camus sees this community [the *pieds-noirs*] as "a people without a past, without tradition."[8] They arrive in Algeria, concludes Sénac, "like the pioneers in America, and—in their moment of joy—they feel the anxiety of being foreign without being able to name it." The psychological state of the colonizer with respect to the colonized (the dialectics of attraction-repulsion) had been conveyed in Camus's fictions (in the early '40s), even though the writer had also condemned the misery in Kabylia and supported the Algerian nationalists during that same period. Fifteen years later, during the Algerian War, one finds every indication that Camus chose to defend the French native land above all, instead of "justice" for the other "Arab" inhabitants, and instead of humanitarian action for the imprisoned Algerian militants.

Finally, Sénac was hoping that a production of *The Stranger* (which he described as a "motionless Western") would take into consideration the political climate of the times, the geographical landscape, and the *pied-noir*

---

* He received Sénac on two occasions, on April 16 and May 18, 1967.

framework, as much as the Arab people "absent present, everywhere active in witnessing but silent." Acting on his ideas, as usual, he takes advantage of Visconti's visit to Algiers, in November 1966, and explains to him all the little-known aspects of *The Stranger*, in particular the sociopolitical context of Algeria between 1935 and 1938, when the narrative takes place. The movie director "took them into consideration, although discreetly" according to Sénac, in a letter he wrote on April 17, 1967,[9] to Mohamed-Seddik Benyahia, a friend of his in Paris at the time of the UGEMA, who later became the minister of Information.

Few are aware that Sénac was named "literary advisor to Mr. Visconti"[10] by the movie's coproducer, Casbah Films, even though his name wasn't included in the credits. In that role, he saw the movie director regularly during the shooting, between November 1966 and February 1967.[11] He collaborated closely on certain aspects of the production: the choice of Camus's apartment in Belcourt, which we see in the first scenes of the movie, and the actor Brahim Hadjaj for the role of the "Arab," who had also played Ali la Pointe in *The Battle of Algiers* (by Gillo Pontecorvo), etc.

The filming of Visconti's *The Stranger* sparked some negative reactions towards Camus, in 1967, among a few Algerians. In his article "Le seul respect que je dois à Camus [The only respect that I owe Camus]," Malek Haddad found it necessary to "demystify a legend that presents this writer as an anti-colonialist craftsman, a servant of Algeria."[12] In a conference given in Algiers on February 10, 1967 (published later in "Au chapitre des remises en question: Albert Camus vu par un Algérien[13] [On the topic of reevaluation: Albert Camus seen by an Algerian])," the minister of Education Ahmed Taleb-Ibrahimi challenged the title of "Camus l'Algérien [Camus the Algerian]" and concluded that he "will remain for us a great writer, if not a great stylist, but still a stranger."

Sénac privately condemned statements made by these two "friends," whom he had met in Paris in January 1955, and who had become staunch adversaries.[14] Simultaneously, he endorsed Laâdi Flici, who, in this harsh environment, delivered a pro-Camus speech—on January 16, 1967, in Algiers (in the Union of Algerian Writers' hall)—that provoked "violent reactions," probably because the speaker declared, "Like Sisyphus, we should imagine a joyful Camus."[15]

Sénac also attended a conference by Emmanuel Roblès[†]—co-screenwriter of the movie with Georges Conchon and Cecchi d'Amico, Visconti's favorite dialogue writer—who focused on issues of fidelity and betrayal between the literary text and the cinematic adaptation.

During this year of 1967, Sénac revived the memory of Camus on three other occasions:

1. On November 21–22, 1966, he completed his study "Notes sur *L'Étranger de Camus*," in which he questioned the general opinion (which he shared as well in his youth)[16] that the novel's writing had been influenced by a so-called American technique: "*The Stranger*'s style, they say "the Americans," you bet, he took it from the *Cagayous*, from the mouth of his mother."[17]

2. In an afterword (dated April 1966–April 1967) he wrote for a new edition of *Soleil sous les armes* (a project that remained unfinished), Sénac provides priceless information on Camus's first meeting with the Muslim Algerian students in October 1955, and on the regrettable quarrel caused by the manifesto, previously examined.

3. On September 1, 1967, Sénac presents "A companion in the night: René Char"[8] for the new radio series *Poésie sur tous les fronts* [Poetry on all fronts],[‡] which he began at the Algerian Radio and Television network in August. As mentioned previously in part 1, Sénac the radio host read from one of Camus's unpublished texts on René Char, not without emotion, as we see in the following statement: "I'm sure that Camus would have been deeply moved that his writings (the aforementioned text, added to Char's writings) are now given back to a new avid audience by young actors from his native land." This emotion is still tangible in two drafts by Sénac, written that same year, 1967: in the first he writes: "All these people who knew him. I spent many intimate hours in his company. He was one of those beings who, in order to show his affection, found the tender and discreet word that would brighten your day"; in the second he reuses

---

† At the French Cultural Center of Algiers, on February 7, 1967.

‡ Following his program *Poète dans la cité* [A poet in the city], from 1964 to 1965.

a passage that he had dedicated to Camus, from a letter that Hölderlin wrote to Schiller: "To Camus. Because I wanted to be everything for you I had to tell myself that I was nothing for you."[19]

In 1970, as his poems of youth, *Les Désordres*, were about to be published—a title that symbolized an era of derangement well—Sénac remembers Camus, "a friendship dismissed for a while,"[20] and restates the note he wrote fifteen years earlier (1955). He also recalls *Noces* and reiterates his fortuitous indebtedness towards its author in an interview given to Jean-Pierre Péroncel-Hugoz.[21]

Finally, in his last article, "L'Algérie, d'une libération à l'autre [Algeria, from one liberation to another]"—published in *Le Monde Diplomatique* in August 1973, a few days before his death—Sénac, once again as Camus's reader, considers that the writings of the Nobel recipient (citing *The Stranger* and *The Plague*) "are for us, on the eve of the *Nahda* (the Renaissance), a crucial hiatus."[22] In hindsight these two texts had become classic references for him, enacting the separation between a French literature in Algeria and an Algerian literature in French, between the old and the new. The issue of terminology, of designating the two literatures was thus resolved.

Sénac's actions and writings after the death of Camus reveal that he never got over their separation. While their differences on the future of Algeria at war were plain and clear (the first saw independence as inevitable, while for the second it was unacceptable), the poet realized that Camus had been correct too soon on the impossible assimilation of the *pieds-noirs* into a new postcolonial city that could only belong to the Arabs and Berbers. The differences between these two cultures and the European community ran too deep.

The hope that Sénac expressed in his writings for a plural Algeria, along with the FLN's warring discourse on the European minority in an independent Algeria,[23] which he expressed in his own writings, quickly turned into disappointment, then into fracture, before ending in nightmare. Every poem he wrote during his last years, published or unpublished,[24] bitterly confirms this. "Citoyens de beauté"[25] [Citizens of beauty] became "Citoyens de laideur"[26] [Citizens of ugliness].

Conclusion

efore the Algerian War, the subject of literature had dominated the friendship between Sénac and Camus, even though politics had already been intruding. In a chronological presentation that includes psychohistory, we've examined the origin and the complexity of Sénac's attitudes towards his friend, both as a writer and as a man. The Algerian War, which pitted them against each other, not only with respect to the predominant policy, but the literature it conditioned, finally split them apart.

Sénac and Camus were tragic figures in their lives as well as in their friendship, the first with outbursts of hope and of despair, the second with moments of happiness. More than the failure of the friendship between men, their breakup confirmed the failure of a literature that addressed the political problems of its time, while being somewhat subservient.

Both literature and politics are the realms of the imaginary, that is, a certain form of a "lie." Sénac remained consistent on this issue: literature is a mission, a "divine"[1] one in its prime, which later supported an Algerian concept, that of the nation's liberation, and which finally contributed to the birth of a new humanity in a new Algeria.

With this literature of the outside, one that must never cheat, the poet allowed for a more intimate expression of quest, in which he sought himself, lost himself, and accomplished himself. From the confrontation of these two trajectories was born his wish to balance, if not to reconcile, politics and love, his historical and his personal truth. This desire was never satisfied, since:

1. Sénac's singularity, both in terms of his intimacy and identity, couldn't triumph over the norms of his newly found countrymen, even if he had predicted in 1954 that "One day I will also have to give my private life to the Nation."[2]
2. It's still difficult to know with certainty whether he was assassinated by politics or by love, since the circumstances of this tragedy have never been elucidated.

On the other hand, Camus's position with respect to literature and politics was contradictory and never clearly stated throughout his career. During his beginnings in Algeria (towards 1935), his political and cultural activism were obvious ("The work is a confession. I have to be witness");[3] during the dark years of Occupied France he was suspicious of the word "literature;"[4] in 1946, after the war, he now was suspicious of all forms of committed literature and declared that he preferred "committed men to committed literature."[5] His distrust for this type of writing was even more apparent during the Algerian War. ("The intellectual . . . [who] takes part in public affairs only through his writing lives like a coward. He compensates his impotence with excessive verbiage.")[6]

Given their stark differences, Sénac and Camus gravitated towards extreme positions and ideas on the Algerian War. This war was their great tragedy, both personally and politically, bringing about the end of a tacit consensus between the son and his father, particularly when faced with the intellectual and with his worldview. Confronted with Sénac's unflinching support of Algeria's independence in his writings and actions, Camus goes from exploring the unspoken to a quasi support of French Algeria. Within these two attitudes we revealed that the gap between the writings and the political convictions (declared or personal) of both men was virtually nonexistent, even if Camus tried to separate them at all cost. Politics, with its hold on human reality, ultimately triumphed over the idealized or deceitful writing of human lives.

In truth, a writer can become the echo of political events given that they are an intrinsic part of his immediate environment. Yet, in order to avoid despair and disillusionment, like Camus in times of war, or Sénac in postcolonial Algeria, he should avoid picking sides—in works that are purely literary—on debates that are subject to powerful and shifting external forces. Given how difficult it is for the writer to apprehend the art of execution in politics, failure is always lurking.

PART III

Correspondence and Radio Shows

Jean Sénac and Albert Camus's Correspondence

The correspondence between Jean Sénac and Albert Camus is deposited at the Jean Sénac Collection of the National Library of Algeria, and at the Mediterranean Collection of the Alcazar Library of Marseille. All of Sénac's letters—actually the drafted minutes of his letters—(except for numbers 33, 34, 36, and 37) are in the first collection, whereas all of Camus's letters (except for numbers 32 and 35) belong to the second. The transcription rigorously follows the script of the original texts, autographed or typed, including the underlined expressions or words.* The time and place of their mailing, when nonexistent or incomplete, are those that appear on the envelopes. Additional information is provided through annotations.

The author wishes to express his warm regards and gratitude to Mrs. Catherine Camus, beneficiary, and to Mr. Jacques Miel, executor of Sénac's estate and beneficiary, for having given their permission for this publication.

■   ■   ■

---

* All italicized words in the correspondence are underlined in the original letters.

1 _____

Sanatorium of Rivet, June 16, 1947

Albert Camus,

I can't call you "Mister," it's too conventional, or "dear friend," too familiar. You don't know me. I know you without having seen you. Lectures, photos, conversations have enabled me to situate the man in his work and his life. So I know you.

Two years ago, in the army, at 18, I discovered *Caligula*, I was enthralled by *The Misunderstanding*. I was told, it was written that *Caligula* is a masterpiece, but that *The Misunderstanding* . . . Maybe . . . I'm not a man of theater nor a critic. When I speak of a work, I can't reason, I can't criticize, I can't attack. I love and I speak of those that I love, of what I love. Maybe it's dumb. This is how I am. After having read *The Stranger*, reread *The Myth of Sisyphus*, passionately loved *Nuptials*—oh, thank you Camus for that little book!—I wanted to write to you. I didn't know how to, didn't dare. What could I say to Camus? My admiration for his work? The joy in how it evolved in me? The vibrations of a heart, of a young soul, thirsty, hesitating, anxious? A momentary hope, rich and dense sustained by Brua's announcement that you were visiting Algiers—which in fact didn't happen? Words, words of a child. Nonsense. And then Roblès, not forgetting Galliéro—(what a great guy, what a man of heart, alive, full, whole, direct, joy in purity, in sincerity, in straightforward and frank affection)—spoke of you again and again. My desire bursts! Here I am. That's all. Fréminville[1] perhaps sent you my poem *Santa Cruz*,[2] which was dedicated to you. It sprang from the source. The rest is not important.

I enjoyed the poems of Blanche Balain. Realities, affinities, rhythms. I will thus speak of them since they grabbed me, moved me, captivated me:

Given with their hands, their eyes, their voice.
Their naked transparent flesh where dreams are seen.

These lines from *Temps lointain* are dedicated to you. Maybe you know their author. Could you give me her address? Héliosang's† daughter can't refuse a meeting with someone she knows well.

> Sad in his drunkenness.
> Alone with his loves.
> Who played out his life in broad daylight.[3]

Will you do this for me?—thank you. Paris, literature, life keeps you busy I'm sure, a minute for the little poet from Oran in a sanatorium as we speak.

I must tell you immediately, I'm Christian, Christian anarchist Roblès once said. "Affinities between me and him? Impossible!" Now don't scream. It's possible since that's the way it is. Next to the Bible—which I sometimes page through—I have in my closet Rilke's *Letters* [*to a Young Poet*] and your *Nuptials*. I don't know what I want? That's also possible. But I'm twenty years old and in love, and in the isolation of the sanatorium I want to smile and laugh and live in hope of honest happiness. The three books I mentioned help me. So I'm not looking for more, or beyond. Should I? It's not important, at least for now.

I saw in the newspaper your added fame: *Prix des critiques*. Bravo. We from Algeria are proud of it. Can you send me *The Plague* when it's published? (I experienced that period in Oran. Speaking of which the Spanish doctor who sounded the alarm wasn't decorated. The medals went to other gentlemen as usual! Stupid.)

I hope to read you. My isolation will be lessened. Here's my picture, on my sanatorium bed reading *Nuptials*. Staged. No! At the time I wasn't thinking of writing you. To write what? To send you that photo why? Do I know? I'm a kid. And I'm thinking: maybe he'll read me. He'll maybe look at that picture before throwing it all in the garbage. Maybe he'll be happy with a little sun and fervor from Africa, from our home?

---

† Héliosang was the name of a poem by Blanche Balain, included in *Temps lointain*. According to Guy Dugas, "It evokes that common space of sun and blood that the young Sénac, Blanche Balain, and before them Camus with his *Nuptials*—to whom the poem was dedicated—were beginning to constitute in their poetry." Sénac's letter was included in an essay by Blanche Balain, published in the review *AWAL*, vol. 10 (1993), Spécial Jean Sénac, 185–189. References, citation, and note from Guy Dugas to the translator.

Goodbye Albert Camus. Thank you with all my heart with joy and hope. Don't begrudge me the use of that anti-absurd word. But to hell with all the formulas since I feel, since I live that word. So, truly yours. Jean Sénac.

PS:
I was going to write to Roy who was really nice to me and thank him for his books. My apologies if you see him. Give him and Fréminville my best regards.[4]

2 _____

Tuesday, June 24 [*1947*]

Dear Sénac,

Yes, you did well to write me. What comes from over there is always dear to me, but what can one say about a 20-year-old friend and poet who is ill like I was in that same heat. Few letters can touch me as much as yours. You'll understand better when you have a clearer idea of what I am, I mean when, forgetting about the little stories of reputation, we can laugh around a drink like we know how to do back home.

I received your letter in a mountain hole where I fled to from Paris. It's a good thing because, in the turmoil of Paris, the heart is no longer free, one answers only halfway. I'm here until July 15th. Write me more about yourself. Are you better? Anyway, I'm not very worried. It's an illness that benefits Algerians. In ten years it has allowed me to produce the work of two men. I believe that we have to keep the strength (isolation and reflection) that it gives and refuse its weaknesses. Forgive me if I'm meddling in things that don't concern me. But, after all, it's what I would tell a younger brother.

Another thing: your poems are not bad. They are sometimes clumsy, unrestrained—but I like the voice that speaks in *Présence*[5] and in *Puissance du rêve*[6] (bad titles but the text rings out). You must continue. Patiently. It takes years to become a writer. You have a gift, that's for sure. It's half. The other half is character and perseverance. I know this because I have only the illusions that I need regarding my work, I have barely begun to know my language (which reminds me, the address of Blanche Balain—30, avenue de Fleurs, Nice [Alpes-Maritimes]). She'll be overjoyed to receive your letter. And she deserves it.

Christian anarchist doesn't bother me. We can accept everything and love everything, aside from murder. This is why it isn't easy to live today. You have two reasons (anarchist and Christian) to reject the philosophies of murder. That's enough for a start.

I wanted to send you *The Plague*. But I don't have any here. I'll have Paris send it to you. I'm including my autograph to this letter. I'll transcribe it to the book when we see each other (I'm going to visit my mother in Algiers, in the fall).

Rest well. Work and be happy. I'm sending you my fraternal thoughts since we are all brothers over there and I shake your hand.

Albert CAMUS.
Le Panelier par Mazet-Saint-Voy (Haute-Loire)[7]

3

Le Panelier, July 13 [*1947*]

My dear Sénac,

I'm returning to Paris in two days, and since I'll be somewhat overwhelmed there, I'm taking advantage of the calm that I enjoy here to write to you. I was glad to receive your letter. I'll be very pleased once I know that you are fully recovered and out of your little cloister (I read in the newspapers that people over there were malnourished and that there were incidents—do you need anything?).

Me, I'm well rested here and the children too (I have twins, boy and girl, who are two years old). I didn't work much, only a little for a play by J. L. Barrault where I wrote the dialogues—a kind of spoken and mimed transposition of *A Journal of the Plague Year*, by Daniel Defoe.

The rest of the time I slept, ate and went trout fishing (don't feel bad for them, I didn't catch any). But now I will put my collar back on since I have my program to finish by spring. I will then probably go to South America if stupidity and hatred haven't swept everything away in the world.

But I will go to Algeria in the fall. I hope that we will be able to see each other and talk a little. I'm going mostly for my mother, who's quite old now.

Rest and work for yourself. I'm thinking of you, very affectionately.

Albert Camus.[8]
My address in Paris: 5, rue Sébastien Bottin (VIIe).

4 ───────────────────────────────────────

[*Paris*], *April 7* [*1948*]

My dear Sénac,

Thank you for your letter and for your poetry. I had already read the complete collection (*Mesure d'homme*),[9] and was further convinced that you have the freshest and most authentic talents. Simply, and as it often happens, those talents come with convenience and you don't make enough *selection*. That's what you need to strive for in my opinion. Leave confession behind, you can come back to it when you're entirely confident in your abilities. When starting on a quest like yours, guided by discipline and technique, confession can lead to abandonment. For the time being you need to hold back your hands. That's my opinion, and you can do what you want with it. There's a certain *naiveté* in you (like how Schiller spoke of the admirable Greek *naiveté*), which is irreplaceable. Knowing how to keep that water clear in the crucible of technique is the practice of the true artist. But in pure water there are only false poets: most of the ones that we admire today.

So long, my dear Sénac. I was happy to meet you. Less so to be back in Paris, its labyrinth and its shabby Minotaur.

Yours, faithfully.

A. Camus.

5 ────────────────────────────────────

[Paris], September 7 [1948]

My dear Sénac,

You were right to respond to Isou[10] if you felt the need to. But you're honoring him greatly. That kind of work isn't worth a penny. They're like cold sores on a sick body. When health returns, the humors disappear. All the provocations in the world can't give Isou any fame, or great talent. He will serve only his publicity, which is not the same thing. Same verdict for *Noir de la vigne*.[11] It's plagiarism of something that isn't even worth plagiarizing. The question, the joy, the real pain are elsewhere.

I prefer to see you write poems. You are moving forward, you're making progress on a difficult road: the right one. Have confidence. If Parain[12] and I spoke a little about you it wasn't because we saw ourselves as "business managers." We felt that we were your comrades, that's all.

Were we talking about money at [Sidi] Madani? I didn't notice it. But life is hard in France. At home poverty is easy. Here it is cold and unforgiving. Sometimes it can kill. One needs compassion.

I have just spent a month in the beautiful countryside of Vaucluse, which looks like ours. I worked there, found an internal leisure there. But I'm leaving for Paris on Friday and the rehearsals for my play at Barrault's are waiting. Hellish work!

So long, my dear Sénac. Work, be happy, you're worth all the Isous in the world, know that. And never doubt my loyal sympathy.

Albert Camus.

6 ───

Algiers, Wednesday, October 26, [19]49

I thought of writing you at greater length, but what more can I say than these poems? Try to read them, dear Camus, I'll be happy. The collection *Genêts, main, plage, et autres mots* [Brooms, hands, beach, and other words] combines texts that are already old, some of them from February 1948.[13] The social, religious, and most importantly verbal concerns of the time provide the frame. Terrible times where words became enemies and, occupying the space, strangled the flesh and the idea. A state of impotence, inability to express, to communicate, I even doubted poetry and its true content. I hardly wrote anymore. For a long time I remained silent. But the physiological need was there, I had to "piss" poems. I interrogated the word, I abused it, I improvised sounds (to at least recognize myself in a warped mirror!). After Eluard I took Artaud as a brother. And the answer appeared on its own (the answer, a temporary answer?) to calm my vanity, that pathological need for the absolute.

I tried to follow your advice: to control myself, to avoid sentimental fusions, to choose. Rigor, tightening, refusing complacency, giving to objects, to sentences a carnal, palpable content, to embody the word, that's what my efforts are reaching for today. I'm very disappointed with the results, but with a little time and a little courage I hope I can find the key and give something worthwhile. See my last things, the *Sensibles*.[14] What do you think? Obvious influence of Char, that great poet, that honest man poised in Speech. I read him every day. I let his work sink in me, roar, yell, march. Wonderful discovery. Mystery and . . . furor. Thank you Camus for having caused that. It's thanks to you, since that evening in Madani when you mentioned it, that I discovered that poetry of man, which teaches me rigor and honesty, truth and modesty. I wrote to Char yesterday (speaking of which, could you send me his exact address?). Four years ago I found my philosopher: Albert Camus. Around the same time came the fruitful revelation of the painter Galliéro, my brother. Today, finally, I discover the poet that I was always searching for: René Char! It's good. Life isn't so dreadful. These lofty friendships can at least ensure one's endeavor.

Summer is ending here. I went swimming, took some exhilarating submarine strolls (with goggles) at Cap Caxine, Palm Beach, l'Ilôt, Matifou. It's my first summer of *Nuptials* (after the war and sickness). I'm trying to make it last. Tomorrow I'm thinking of going to the pier to "take a swim." The days are mild, filled with screams, smells, as though invaded with tenderness. Monday, I presented a study of you on the radio, "Poète de la joie de vivre" and a montage of your texts "Noces avec le monde [Nuptials with the world]." A true symphony of earthly joy. Were you able to listen to it? I'll send you a copy of the show. I already recorded it (in case you couldn't listen to it).

Lately I reread *The State of Siege* (used extensively in the show), which continues to enthuse me despite the "dissatisfied." One of your old acquaintances from Oran let me borrow *Betwixt and Between*. I'm deeply moved by that imperfect book, particularly the passage where you spoke of your mother. It reminds me somewhat of my own and of myself. I think you're going to make me do something "ugly" (?): I'm going to ask this lady to give me a copy of your book; if she refuses, if feel like I'll . . . (unless I take a typed copy!).

What are you up to? The Radio's maybe sending me . . . to Paris for a workshop in a few months. I hope that I can join you, enter the jungle, work seriously, enrich myself, decant. Anyway, if the Radio keeps me here without a plan, I ditch everything and split. It's becoming necessary. I'll manage over there. Fundamentally, I believe that one must trust life. One always pulls through. Who would that Christian be if he doubted the Word: "Ask and you shall receive."

I read *Empédocle* regularly, and find there my beloved writers, Grenier among others.

My best regards to Jules Roy, to Parain and his lady. My respects to Madame Camus. Write to me, tell me honestly what you think of my poems. Your critiques are precious to me. Be harsh and demanding, you owe it to the infinite admiration, to the affection I have for you. Thank you. Could you suggest two or three texts that I could send to Jean Vagne?[15]

I would like to give you some sun, ours. Fullheartedly, your

Jean Sénac.

PS:
I would appreciate it if you could return *Genêts, main, plage*, after reading it. So long.

7

[*Paris*], *November 7* [*1949*]

My dear Sénac,

A brief note. I'm in bed, and for quite a long time. It's an illness that you know well.

I couldn't hear anything only gurgling sounds from your two recordings. Send me the transcripts, it will distract me. And thank you!

What is more important: your poems. You have made *great progress*. I was pleased with them, so pleased that I thought we should try to make your voice known. Let me choose something and send it to Jean Vagne for *Empédocle.*

Carry on and carry on with resolve. Refuse that which is pretty or affectionate. Besides you have a heart. There will be plenty of it left in what you write. But it's also true that you have a talent that doesn't owe anything to anyone, luminous and healthy, with real courage.

So long, my dear Sénac. I shake your hand, affectionately.

A.C.

Don't take too many sun baths if you don't want to have another go at that thing [tuberculosis].

8

[*Paris*], *December 16* [*1949*]

My dear Sénac,

Yes, publish your collection.[16] The selection seems good to me. Add to it "Miroir de l'Eglantier [Mirror of the brier]."[17] If you come to Paris in January I'll be in the mountains. But I'll let my secretary know, Ms. Suzanne Labiche, NRF [Nouvelle

Revue Française], 5 rue Sébastien Bottin. Write to her about your arrival and she'll find a room for you. Wear warm clothes and everything should be ok. The weather in Paris is good, although sometimes rough.

As for the advertisement, you can probably find a couple of lines in one of my letters. If I could think and work, I would send you a more adequate text soon.

Your loyal
A.C.

9

[*Cabris (Alpes-Maritimes), May 27, 1950*][18]

Still resting. Will try sending you text, if I can work. Think before going to Paris. If you do decide to go, let me know so that I can have friends welcome you there. Your poems are beautiful, and I'm glad.

Affectionately.
Camus.

10

Algiers, August 1, 1950

My dear Camus,

I just obtained the General Government's literary grant (with Galliéro for painting). My desire to come to Paris is materializing. I'm going to resign from the Radio. I'm thinking of leaving Algiers on August 14 or 16.

I will spend a few days in Lourmarin, in the Vaucluse. I can take that opportunity to meet Char in Isle sur Sorgue. I would like to see you as well. Where are you staying at the moment? Then I'll dash off to Paris where I'll try to find a room (can I still ask Suz[anne] Labiche to find one for me?). I'm leaving with about two or three months of savings (75,000 F). Towards November I'll look for a menial job. I'm determined this time. Now that the Lourmarin Grant gives me the means to leave, I no longer hesitate. I have a lot to learn in Paris and I really need that *choc*, that wonder and the hard trial no doubt of lost illusions. I was told that fall there is magical.

I'm thinking of a novel on Oran during the American occupation: an adolescent struggling in the midst of tragedy and carnival. Theater also (a Christian faced with Peace and Murder and an evangelical transposition). And so many things to cough up, to get out, there, with some hindsight. I need another environment, other people, other times, to flee from my past a little, to decant, to find myself, to sing this land that clogs my pores, this wonderful ocean, these tough and healthy people with whom I proudly share the journey. I must also abandon my mother.

I'm socializing a lot these days, Communist friends, PPA or UDMA. We often meet on the pier or in the Casbah. This year Ramadan had a profound meaning. We are witnessing an awakening. I know that I need Paris. But I will come back in a year or two. We have so much work to do here. Maybe we can't reach for the moon but there are still a few human values we can save, defend, in the great chaos that's coming.

Goodbye Camus. Be happy. Keep on conquering. May the summer not make you as foolish as me. Can you send me your current address (in the mountains or at Cabris?) and tell me if it's possible to come and see you? I know that it will help me a lot before Paris. Many thanks. Affectionately. Jean Sénac.

My best regards to your family.[19]

11

[*Gérardmer (Vosges)*], *August 12* [*1950*]

Dear Sénac,

I won't be in Paris until September 1st. Suzanne Labiche (who's now Agnely through marriage) won't be there until the 19th. But write to the Hôtel de l'Académie, rue des Saints-Pères, Paris 6th [arrondissement], *on my behalf* to reserve a room. It will be a temporary arrangement for you, on the rive gauche, in a friendly neighborhood, and less expensive. We'll see when I get back. You can have your meals (delicious!) at the hotel and Mrs. Millet, the owner of the place, will take care of you. In case there's no room, write to Hôtel de la Minerve, 22 rue de la chaise, Paris 7th. I've stayed there. Prices are average.

I'm in the Vosges, traveling around, and you might miss me. The best is that we meet in Paris. I hope that you'll be happy there, even though the city's all-consuming. But you're not arriving alone—and you will have help. See you soon. It rains here, almost all the time. I sleep and I work, that's my schedule.

Affectionately yours.
Camus.

Soleil is very good. I haven't forgotten that I owe you a text. You'll have it in Paris. And for the rest, good luck! Write me, 17, rue de l'Université, and it will be forwarded.

12 _____

[Algiers], Thursday, August 17 [1950]

My dear Camus,

Thank you for everything that your letter brings to me.

Yes, I want to be happy there, which means stronger than the disappoint-ments and the failures. I will try to bring a temperamental, lazy kid that I am, on the threshold of manhood with his responsibilities, his audacity, his necessary pride and humility. I have so much to learn and I've already lost many friends.

I'm happy to learn that *Caligula* is returning this season. Tonight I must pick up your *Actuelles* at Charlot's.‡ It will be my travel companion. I've been captivated by *L'Enracinement* [*The Need for Roots*] these past few days.[20] After such a deep progression, one feels small and "unaccomplished."

I've just spent two days at Rivet where I saw my friends again.

I'm taking the boat on August 23rd and am thinking of spending about a week in Provence. I'll be in Paris at the end of the month. I'll probably go to Hôtel de l'Académie.

Thanks again and see you soon. I'm hoping that you'll find some sun.

Wholeheartedly.
J. Sénac.

PS: "Here are some fruit [not yet, of course!], some flowers, some leaves." A few recent things.

_____

‡ Edmond Charlot, born in Algiers, began his bookstore Les Vraies Richesses in 1936. He published many young Algerian writers, including Camus's first work in 1937.

13
_____

L'Isle, September 13, 1950[21]

I've just spent a wonderful week with Char. A prince in his domain, of love and of the seasons. Thank you Camus for introducing me to this man. He's Purification and Promise, prestigious simplicity. A poet irrigated with vital blood, his trees, his water put poetry in its place . . . I'm coming up to Paris armed, dissident, and happy. Against the darkest hour I still have that small island, the friendship of a few, yours and the hope of an imperishable sun. With these one can face the labyrinth. So long.

Sénac.

14
_____

[Paris], April 27 [1951]

My dear Sénac,

I'm glad that things are going well for you. You feel that you are being badly treated, while within yourself you were treating others poorly. The sky of Paris has some wicked spells. Children and flowers, these are worth it. But I can't tell it well, perhaps I can speak of it better. To live is hard, that's for sure.

I'm working a lot. Stop by the NRF, towards noon, and we'll have a drink. Don't think that I'm forgetting you. But I'm all alone with too many things to take care of. Up to now I haven't found any help.

You're right to publish *Arbre*, it's a beautiful collection.[22]

Affectionately yours.
Albert Camus.

15 _____

[Paris], July 13 [1951]

My dear Sénac,

The Rockefeller Institute, in New York, is offering travel grants to young Algerian intellectuals. They asked Jean Grenier to draft a short list. I gave your name to Grenier and I hope that it's ok with you. If not you can always refuse.

As for the rest, never mind. What little I've said should be enough to dispel a slight misunderstanding. I know what life is like, and that it's not easy. Nevertheless you are privileged, as I was in Prague. There are difficult privileges, that's all. But those are the ones that held me, and that will keep you standing.

Affectionately yours,
Albert Camus.

16 _____

[Paris], July 25 [1951]

Dear Sénac,

I'm leaving tonight unfortunately and will be back towards the 10th of September. Call me then and we'll have a longer conversation.

Your friend, A. Camus.

17 _____

[*Paris*], *X 31* [*19*]*52*

My dear Sénac,

I was waiting for some news regarding the collection in order to write you. I reviewed it and requested its publication. But we need a second reader, as you know. And he's not in any hurry. Therefore, let's wait.

I'll send you a text, of course. But why the *NRA*, since you don't want to ape Paris.[23] And beware of two dangers: "literature" around the Mediterranean (not too much) and political "colonization," whether direct or indirect, of the Right or of the Left. Your review will succeed only if it's in firm hands: the least amount of words, maximum efficiency and *no* concessions.

I'll be in Algiers at the end of November. We'll have time to talk about all that. Don't regret Paris, green and gray.

Faithfully yours.
Camus.

18 _____

[*Paris*], *Monday 24* [*of December 1952*]

Dear friend,

Baya[24] is in very good hands. Her show is a success and a well-earned one. I've often admired the kind of miracle expressed in each of her works. It's a joy for the eyes and the heart in this dark and frightened Paris. I also admired the disdain in her posture among the crowd at the opening: she was the princess among barbarians.

In any case thank you for having introduced me to her. As for the rest, don't worry.

Your faithful

Albert Camus.[25]

19 _____

[Paris], Thursday, February 12, 1953

My dear Sénac,

Your book was accepted, after some (long) hesitation. I've taken it into my collection, which will solve everything. But there will be a small delay in production. In any case, you are now free from that concern—and I hope that this will give you back the smile that you lost.

Terrasses. If you can wait a few days, I will give you a fairly long text (a dozen typed pages), "Retour à Tipasa [Return to Tipasa]" that I prize and that also takes a "position" albeit in a purely literary fashion. I'm working on it now and it should be ready relatively soon.

The summary seems good. Be careful with chronicles and notes—which don't tolerate mediocrity.

Something else: send me *by return mail* the manuscript of my piece on Char, which you kept. A small German press asked me for a short introduction on Char, and I might find a few elements there. If you want to keep the manuscript I will have it typed and will return it to you. *But it's urgent.*

So long. Affectionately.

Albert Camus.

20

[Paris], Tuesday [March 3, 1953]

Dear Sénac,

I was almost going to call to tell you to *Leave me alone,* as one might say to friends who don't understand that I'm working for them. Because I've been working for you, and tirelessly, for the past 15 days and your letter arrives in the middle of work precisely and delays me instead of hurrying things up.

Had you a quarter of my hassles, you would be more patient. With this work, even these delays, I'll give you the best opening piece that I can give you today. I've rewritten this text four times. I'm having it typed tonight. You'll receive it *Monday* at the latest. But calm down and don't make it a persecution. Every promise you were given so far was kept. And! no the piece is late. But is this shipment of fuel or of molasses!

Send me the proofs, which I'll correct in 24 hours. Ah! How I dislike working for reviews, even Algerian ones. If you fully realized, you would write me in a different way. The convent, that's what I want.

Affectionately.
A.C.

21

[Paris], Thursday [May 3, 1953]

Dear Sénac,

Here you go. I would have rewritten it again, if I had the time. But one has to stop somewhere. Send the proofs. And good luck!

A. C.

22

No date [April 25, 1953]

Dear Sénac,

Here are the proofs, much corrected. But the printer has his share of responsibility. Please oversee the corrections, so that they don't lead to more mistakes.

I liked your texts, for the most part. Tighten up, tighten yourself up, stand up straight. Yes, everything is difficult, and you're following paths that I once followed. But you have to clench your teeth and move on, without expecting anything in return, above all with no expectation.

Affectionately.
A. Camus.

23

Paris, July 3, [19]53[26]

My dear Sénac,

A very brief word since I'm particularly tired lately and am forced to take some time off. TERRASSES presents itself well. You need to work on the chronicles and notes section, and be very demanding. But this first issue is really satisfying. I can't promise anything for the next issue: I'm really too tired.

Yours, very affectionately,
Albert Camus.

Do you happen to have two or three copies of the first issue.

24_____

[*Paris*], [*September 29, 1953*][27]

Dear Sénac,

Thank you for your poems. Several of them are beautiful. Don't think too much of the *maquis* [the armed struggle]. It's easier to dream of it than to return from it, or even to see it coming.

I'll be in Algiers, probably towards January and hope that I'll see you there.

So long.
A. C.

25_____

Paris, November 26, [*19*]*53*[28]

Dear Sénac,

I haven't heard anything on TERRASSES but I hope that the second issue will come out. I'm told that your poems will be published in the spring (April May). It's a good time of the year to bloom.

Affectionately.
Albert Camus.

26_____

Paris, March the 2nd, 1954[29]

Dear Sénac,

Thank you for keeping me up to date. Roblès had already done so. I thought that it was about literature. The least one can say is that it's not entirely clear.

That said, you should have limited yourself to information in your letter. First of all, the word compromise is too much; secondly, I cannot let you write such things about Jules Roy, who's my friend. He can be wrong, he makes mistakes like everybody, like all of you, but I believe that none of you have the right to use the word denunciation. Tell it clearly to all of our friends.

As for the rest, I'm worried that by removing myself from this jury I will upset a lot of good people, but I do so without hesitation. In this case as in so many others, it's true nevertheless that those who criticize me the most are those who are least critical of themselves. It's the law of nature.

Yours, always affectionately.
Albert Camus.

27_____

[Paris], June 18, 1954

Dear Sénac,

Congratulations on the publication of your poems. Thank you too for your card. I don't have the leisure (in the heart) to truly write to you. But my thoughts are with you and I (earnestly) wish you success.

Affectionately.
Albert Camus.

28

Algiers, July 27, 1954.

My dear Camus,

Thank you for my book. I'm happy. I had expressed my joy in a letter to you, but I tore it up, too exalted and childish. In any case I embrace you, big serpentine brother.

L. G. Gros, from *Cahiers du Sud*, sent me a beautiful review in a letter that I'm proud of.[30] You'll see it. I can't subscribe to *Argus*. Could you notify me of any reviews of my book, if any? I'm not harboring any illusions, but still . . .

Otherwise, I have to come up to Paris in a month. It's becoming impossible for me to stay here, I no longer have any real job or home. All I have left is the warmth of my friends, the sun, the sea, and poems. It's a lot, and yet . . . In Paris I'll have work (through "realist" friends). I also hope to make connections, see art shows, performances, and tear myself away from the luxurious comfort of this country where even misery is opulent. You know it.

I asked for an advance of 60,000[§] francs from Gallimard. Is it crazy? Could you help me? It's critical for me. Thank you.

I'm writing a lot. I'm doing the final edits for three poetry collections (including Élégies that I think are better than my *Poèmes*).[31] I'm also finishing my essay on Oran,[32] and my writings on Algiers and the beaches for the rich and the poor here. I haven't wasted my time in the sun. But the narrow-mindedness and the jealousy of my "colleagues" here is revolting. Even so, these people are great and beautiful. I live with them in Bab-el-Oued, in the Casbah and in the sea.

I'm very, *very* poor, and crazier than ever. I hope that Gallimard won't refuse. But I'm happy, *very* happy, terribly strong.

I'm sending you a sheaf of wrasse, of sea urchins, of sun and affection.

Jean Sénac.

---

§ 350 FRF to 1 USD in 1950, which means about $170.

Enclosed are some poems, always.

In this great concern for myself I haven't asked about you. But I'm sending you strong, very strong wishes.

29

[*Paris*], [*August 8, 1954*][33]

Dear Sénac,

Don't "come up" to Paris without certainties and beware of "realist" friends. Gallimard will never advance 60,000 francs to you for poems. If you sold 200–300 copies it would be a success and would guarantee you 10,000 or 15,000 francs in royalties. You need a job, a position, something safe. That said, those who have read your *Poèmes* like them, and for good reason.

Affectionately yours.
A.C.

30

Paris, January 1, 1956

My dear Camus,

After a sinister Christmas, I'm starting the new year in excellent condition. I finally have an independent and comfortable room at 63, rue des Saints-Pères. I can work. I have my energy back. All that thanks to you. I was on the edge of bitterness and the worst idiocies. You pulled me out of a tight spot. Tonight, I celebrated Christmas. Thank you my friend, my teacher (despite the thistles), a very big thank-you. And my wishes, my sincere wishes to you and to those you love.

At Notre-Dame, a little while ago I prayed for you and your family. I was happy crossing through Paris. That hadn't happened to me in so long . . .

Here is a letter that René Char wrote to me concerning *The Rebel.*[34] It's one of the things I treasured most in the world. Please accept my gratitude and my affection.

Enjoy the first morning of the year!

My strong and faithful hand, truer than my words.
J. S.

31

Paris, November 14, 1956[35]

Dear Albert Camus,

We tried to see you. It was impossible. We thought then that we should write you. We deferred that letter for several months. We suffered as a result, since for us there can be no friendship without rigorous honesty. But we respected your silence and tried to quiet within us the questions that it raised.

Today you enter the public arena, concerning Hungary, all enlightened with Insistence and Honesty. Indeed, Hungary is close, but in Algeria our blood is shed every day. The French blood, the Arab blood, whatever, the blood of men! All this at home, Camus, at home.

You know that every day men, women, and children—and very often innocent people—are tortured, imprisoned in actual extermination camps, massacred! We are keeping at your disposal—in case you don't have it already—documentation that you can authoritatively verify with the official agencies.

Against this universe of concentration camps, against this everlasting crime, you have the right, Camus, to raise your voice and to put up your barricades. In Algeria, in each of those men, it's the hope of our friend Jean de Maisonseul that is pilloried. We can no longer remain silent. If we call upon you it's because our voice wouldn't carry beyond a small circle of friends; it's because here, aside from all politics, it's about choosing sides, about condemning the infamy and about defending the simple and painful dignity of both the French and the Algerians.

Your solidarity can't be only for Europeans. And if it's true that you felt closer to a Kabyle shepherd than to a Northern coal miner, oh Camus, speak beyond the injustices, the parties, and demand that the French intellectuals and officials shed full light on the systematic extermination and the daily tortures.

After those interventions you can intensify your resentment toward us. Nevertheless you should know that if Scipio speaks to you again with such violence it's because he refuses to join Chaerea.

As you said in *Le Figaro*, on November 11: "The signatories are assuring you that their call wasn't inspired by any intention—a pretty vain one—to blackmail, but by the painful awareness of their responsibilities and by their anguished rebellion in the face of a people's tragedy."

And when the correspondent for the objective, honest newspaper *Le Monde* speaks of the reaction of the Algerian crowd, I would like him to give me clarifications and information on the ethnic makeup of that crowd.

We give you a strong handshake.
Jean Sénac–Jean Négroni

32

Paris, February 10, 1957[36]

My dear Sénac,

I assume that it is you who requested that your article in *Exigence* be sent to me. I'm surprised however to find in it a note that merits my response, even though I decided to remain silent with respect to Algeria, so that I don't further contribute to its misfortune or to the idiocies that are being written about it. I remind you of your note: "He who writes will never live up to those who die,

Camus once said, at a time when he hadn't yet repudiated the injustice of *The Just.*" That "not yet" is excessive. The subject of *The Just* is precisely what concerns us today and I still think what I thought then. The hero of *The Just* refuses to throw his bomb when he sees that in addition to killing the grand-duke, which he had accepted, he risked killing two children. That refusal, that passionate conviction that there is a limit that shouldn't be crossed in murder and injustice were given as examples, in my play and in *The Rebel*, because to me they are the only ones that can preserve the essence and dignity of rebellion. My position on that topic hasn't changed, and if I can understand and admire the liberation fighter, I have only contempt for the killer of women and children. The cause of the Arab people in Algeria was never harmed more than by the civil terrorism that is now being systematically practiced by the Arab movements. And this terrorism delays, perhaps irreparably, the solution of justice that will eventually intervene.

The objection claiming that the French do the same could be usefully discussed if Arab intellectuals or officials had condemned these murders of innocents just as we did, and publicly, against collective punishment. That wasn't the case. We were then left with our good intentions while they were shooting on [*incomplete sentence, added in handwriting*] If at least you didn't have me agree, even if it's in the past, with actions that disgust me. Instead of denying it, I continue, on the contrary, to condemn in absolute terms, today as I did yesterday, the murder of innocent civilians. I will finally add that your "not yet" isn't just incorrect, it's slightly insulting to a man who you know was the only one of his type, in Algeria, to defend the Arab people twenty years ago.

Indeed I have no lessons to give you. Still let me tell you that I continue to believe that the one who writes never lives up to those who die. Many people today are dying in Algeria, and on both sides. You who write, give it some thought, before pretending, against me, that you accept the infamous injustice of the just. While trivial here, the phrase is worth its weight in blood over there. All that a writer must do, as long as he is not fighting, is be careful not to add to this weight of blood when giving into the ease of language.

Yours,
A.C.

33 _____

[*Florence, September 26, 1957*]³⁷

Despite the falling out, despite the crimes of the Masters of the Vine, the terrible anger of my brothers, despite the night of blood that has engulfed us, I know that one day, together, we will find again the fraternal peace of Fiesole, the peace that I loved before finding it in the pages of *Nuptials*.

[Jean Sénac]

34 _____

Paris, December 18, 1957

Albert Camus,

After reading your letter published in tonight's *Le Monde*, I've taken back the attached article that *France Observateur* was going to publish.

The text was something of a "parricide" to me. It's with relief that I cancel its publication. But this doesn't essentially change anything in our particular positions, nor the certainty that I know some of the deep reasons for your silence.

There. It had to be said. I have tried to contact you several times, in vain. I thought that you were a man of dialogue. I have written you a 30-page letter that I never sent. All this is so useless . . . It's why I decided to speak publicly. Beyond our little ambitious selves are others, and we speak for them. One day I will undoubtedly pursue that article more seriously. I must. I'm going to publish a paper, in *L'Action*, on "the Algerian intellectuals and the revolution"³⁸—where I speak of nonviolence and again of you (but only concerning that single question).

If I'm not in the mountains, the *Maquis*, it's because they rejected me three times. But I serve my people in my own way (a people of nine million

Arabo-Berbers and a million Europeans and Jews). I try to serve love and not hatred, at the very heart of violence.

I know that I am loyal to both the oppressed Arabs and the blinded Europeans. Our face is not that of despair, of unhappiness maybe, but also that of unshakable hope. And already, a number of young European Algerians are preparing the stones of the city with our brothers in combat, each in his own modest way, even my mother has joined me in hope. It's one of the biggest joys of my life. The word has therefore become flesh and lives among us. The others will come, I'm sure. We will vanquish through trust, through love despite the appearances.

No, I am not following anyone's command. I'm not "from the FLN." It's my own solidarity, my hard honesty. I'm on the margin. I'm not part of the feast. I reread *Les Feuillets d'Hypnos* too often to be duped by the powerful of this world![39]

Tomorrow in Algiers, it's Jean Daniel that will be welcomed with great ceremony in the independent Republic, and you, Albert Camus. Not me. Even if I have the joy of seeing my people finally free. I have chosen poetry, frankness, with everyone, love and not masks.

But already the youth are with me, love me. Others will be born that will know me. My victory is not of this world. But of this world are my struggle and my fraternity!

I try to defend together my mother and justice.

In my first letter to you, 11 years ago, I wrote that that I was a Christian anarchist. Today that statement makes me smile. But there's a baptism there, a spiritual order to which I remain loyal, especially since I have a better understanding of what that tiny word *Algerian* means and the commitment that it demands from us.

Jean Sénac.

35

[Paris], December 19, [19]57

What *haste*, Sénac! That nice prosecution, based on hearsay, unfathomable for anyone who knows me a little, and before I was even able to correct myself, is certainly not that of friendship, even a sad one. I was lucky that my correction was published in time, sparing me the sight of your name at the end of *that*, and in *France Observateur*. But I wasn't lucky enough to preserve in you the simple memory, concerning you and concerning the Algerian people. Too bad. At least accept one last advice from your friend: if you continue to speak of love and of fraternity, do not write any more poems glorifying the bomb that indiscriminately kills the child and the dreadful "blind" adult. That poem, which continues to weigh heavily on my heart, took away any value to your arguments, so little assured I am of the value of my own.

Good luck!
Albert Camus.

36

Paris, December 24, 1957

Albert Camus,

Before we become engulfed once again in the thick silence of our small convulsive prides, and maybe because all this is part of an impossible friendship (an "impossible love" as we say), I would also like to correct a few things.

And first of all, that poem that you deem "written in honor of the bomb." How poorly you read it, Camus! Or too quickly. It's true that you are very busy. But what, I reread *Diwan de l'État-Major*[40] and, luckily, I can't find what you're seeing in it. Yes, I spoke of the bomb. The poem is there—on the page that you probably dog-eared—but as a *fact* and not as a tribute. A painful fact without a doubt: "Terrorists, mutilated smile!" And why did you isolate that poem from a collection that is but a single and dreadful attempt at hope (to such an extent that I refused to title those poems and numbered them instead, like the cries of a very long night, with all of its facets, its heaps of depression and its surges of dignity)? Yes, there were times when even I was tempted to push the pain and the nausea to the point of "killing" with the Word. But in that whole book (of 110 poems), there are only two or three rages of that kind. And everything else rejects them.

Why didn't you want to read and understand this call:

Captain Alexander[¶]
can one say "yes" to the deaths of others and live?
Is it possible to live
with that rumor in our blood?
"In the face of everything, ALL THAT
a Colt, the promise of the rising sun!"[41][**]
The sun remains pure on the chief's face,
but the trigger in me mutinied childhood
and no summer will seize upon this frost

I think it's clear and that there's no acceptance or "glory" there.

The dreadful climate of exasperation that the Algerians were plunged into after one hundred years of rejected friendship, of exploited patience, of betrayed hope, has pushed them to their limits I believe—including the political leaders (who under these circumstances are reacting like the rest of the people, with terrible honesty, a furious and honest innocence)—and to respond to the endless lies and calculated crimes with a kind of rage, a deadly embrace (there's "unrequited love" in this tragedy, a kind of sacred jealousy). It's why I cannot condemn the Revolution, any more than I can my friend in Bab-El-Oued who lynches and massacres an "Arab" following the explosion of

---

[¶] René Char's code name, as captain of the French Resistance during WWII.

[**] Translated by Mary Ann Caws and Nancy Kline in *Furor and Mystery and Other Texts.*

the Casino de la Corniche. They are in the grip of a "human" passion that can no longer worry about morals (which we haven't bothered to teach them anyway).

Victim, also, is the reenlisted soldier who responds with fierce cruelty to the death of his friend (no doubt caused by a "pacifying" operation), mutilated in a fierce repression. And victim as well that young paramilitary man in desperate need of action, of physical exploits and even of noble ideals constantly betrayed by the French political climate, and who was exploited by the police. The real torturers, the guilty (for there is a hierarchy, Camus, and crucial distinctions), we know them: they're the exploiters, the corrupt power-hungry, the crazed coward, the mediocre, the kings Borgeaud, Blachette, Schiaffino, Bidault, Morice, Lejeune, Soustelle, Mollet, Lacoste, Juin and most of all Alain de Sérigny and all those who have the mission to inform and awaken.

Our duty is to name those people, to reveal their dreadful machinations even if it doesn't look pretty in the panoply of the true great artist.

Yes, but what about the FLN you ask? Whether you like it or not, that movement today represents the Algerian anger, the longing for freedom and happiness among the intellectual elites, for the elites as well as for the popular masses. It's up to us to preserve and to bring the necessary values for all action. Up to us above all to bring revolutionary thought back to the pinnacle where it belongs. It's our modest work in our modest place. How can you not understand it, you who once reprimanded me so strongly (in the presence of Guilloux and Daniel) for not participating in the Parisian literary world? Yes, there is a bet to be made, but only with a "trust in the Arabs" (their voice, their desire for democracy and true justice) that you don't seem to have.

I will one day pursue my article on you (which contains, I admit, some hasty inferences—and there is, right now, an urgency that displeases me). For quite a while I've been rereading all of your writings on the issue (the older ones from *Alger Républicain*, the more recent ones, some letters, your books). And I always notice the tragic back and forth, the contradictions, the misunderstanding, the ambiguity of words that are simultaneously those of an honest man and of an unforgivable "con-man" ["louette" in Pied-noir] whose register is too vague to produce any melody. Even if you refuse it, you are supporting a policy and have been for a year and 8 months. Exactly like Messali (painful and declining case). And by skirting the Reason of State you risk joining the same people that you despise. That the President of the Court never received a single "confidential" letter from you (Ben Sadok your reader, who admired you and whose life was at stake, Camus!), you the author of *The Just*, is unforgivable (you were undoubtedly aware of Ben Sadok's harrowing scruples—or those of Abderrahmane Taleb, sentenced to death three times in Algiers—and his respect for human life, his effort to strike only Chekkal[††]). Just as painful, for a student at the Faculty of Algiers, to process the following answer: "No, there isn't any discrimination between Arabs and French at the University of Algiers, but there is a factual *numerus clausus* because they are poorer." Because . . . what? You know well that, on the contrary, most Arab students of Algiers are precisely the sons of the rich! Excusing France at all costs is normal for a Nobel recipient who's abroad, less so for the author of *The Plague*.

What is this "homeland" you say you would like to return to together with Kessous?[‡‡] And in that homeland aren't you forgetting 10 million frustrated individuals, rejected by 40 million residents on one hand, a million Europeans on the other, among whom the most innocent, the best almost always side with Borgeaud and Soustelle?

Aren't you forgetting most importantly that those men aren't "without a past," and neither are their cities? Have you considered the harm you have done to them by praising the Roman Algeria, by neglecting that real Algeria, overwhelmingly Arab and Berber? And how! Did the aftermath of your civil truce project not open your eyes? On one hand, Lacoste, who has the following answer for Jean de Maisonseul, "Those issues don't interest me. I wage wars!" On the other, the FLN sector of Algiers was open to discussing the truce and Miquel was going to give you all the information, as well as Jean de Maisonseul during their stay in Paris. They didn't, fearing that they would bother and inconvenience you at the time of the Nobel Prize. I believe that today they finally decided and went ahead because it is crucial and serious.

The real problem for an Algerian today (and there's only one problem, not two!) is:

---

†† Ali Chekkal, former vice president of the Algerian assembly and supporter of Franco-Muslim friendship, was assassinated by Ben Sadok.

‡‡ Aziz Kessous, an Algerian socialist and former member of the Party of the Manifesto.

- What will Algeria become in the coming years (for this, one has to study the international situation, the French situation, the economic and political facts, and even base intrigues)?
- How will the Arab Berbers and the European Algerians live together?
- How can we, as of now, give democracy, justice and fraternity the best chances in Algeria?
- How can we achieve this in the quickest and best way possible?

My decision is warranted, among other things, by the answers I could provide to those questions. However, I saw that independence was inevitable and that its most serious vehicle, for the past three years and until further notice, was without a doubt the FLN. I concluded that I had to reconsider the meaning of my solidarity with my community and the meaning of my attachment to France. There.

I fear that, in the end, your concept of solidarity could lead to a new spirit of nihilism and could render a fatal disservice to your family, to your mother.

I must tell you again that I always safeguard "the simple memory" in me, whatever you might think. It's also because of this simple memory that Simone Weil didn't want to be baptized and why she subscribed to Léon Bloy's statement: "An obedient son of the Church, I'm nevertheless in eager communion with all those who are outraged, disappointed, deceived, all the wretched of this world."

Here's Christmas, a Christmas that for us will never end: "Peace on earth to men of good will!" Nothing can tarnish that hope: neither the misery of the barn, nor the massacre of innocents, or the renunciation, or the cross, or the Father's doubt.

Since Christmas is here, why don't you read the story of Noël Favrelière.[42] He's the purest of your heroes, the saint that you dream of. Or is he also engulfed in your silence?

Happy New Year! On that note let's stop [*illegible word, crossed out*] and everyone shut up, including the abbot in charge of the contracts.[43]

Jean Sénac (in attachment a press clipping from *La Tribune du Peuple* of December 21, 1957).

37

[*Paris*], *April 29, 1958*

Camus

Our brother Taleb was just guillotined. They couldn't get Djamila Bouhired and Henri Alleg. They took vengeance on the most vulnerable, the most noble, the most pure. Taleb was a modern brother of Kaliayev. I know how much I irritate you, but what! Didn't I promise to myself that I would be unbearably frank with you? Couldn't you *demand* student Taleb's pardon from those who would like you to be the Nobel Prize of Pacification?[§§] Had you used your fame for that purpose only, you would have reclaimed it with renewed strength and given it a clear face.

Of course, it's none of my business. Maybe I'm just a huge pain in the ass who thinks he has a conscience . . .

Nevertheless, I'm no longer alone. Fifty Algerian students (of European descent and from all walks of life), amongst thousands, are with me today (here, with difficulty, and not in the euphoria of Tunis). With our Arab Berber brothers we have pledged to serve love, and thereby not only the Algerian people but also the European minority mesmerized by its own suicide.

Abderrahmane Taleb was of those who believed in this community, who did everything to serve it until the last second. Every time a student of that caliber falls, a little bit of our hope is threatened. That's why you, you in particular, had to save that virtuous man and prepare less ominous days for us, tomorrow, when we will be held accountable and when the pure, the fraternal will no longer be able to testify against despair and vindictive mindsets.

At least, our trust remains. There are many Talebs left in the Algerian Revolution. Maybe we'll help build that Republic of Saint-Just that France failed and that I was still dreaming about a few days ago with René Char.

Jean Sénac.

[§§] This refers to the French "pacification" campaigns during the Algerian War where Algerians were massacred, imprisoned, and tortured. Sénac used this reference disparagingly concerning Camus's Nobel Prize.

Two Shows from Radio Algeria, Produced by Jean Sénac

T he typed copies of the radio shows are deposited at the Jean Sénac Collection of the National Library of Algeria [Bibliothèque nationale d'Algérie]. The titles of Sénac's shows often vary, and his productions have transposable titles and subject matters, or are formally grouped together under the general title "Spoken words and music [*Paroles et musiques*]" or "Men and literature [*Hommes et lettres*]." The words and expressions in italics are underlined in the typed manuscript.

Literary program: "A poet of the joie de vivre: Albert Camus" (*Monday October 24, 1949, at 8:30 p.m.*)

[*Reading of long passages from* Nuptials]

Philosopher of the absurd, Albert Camus denies being a poet. "I often have the (humiliating) feeling that I don't understand anything about poetry." Indeed, his concern for clairvoyance and clearheadedness could justify this attitude. The poet is an exalted being, but even if he accepts the craziest ideas, as an unrepentant gambler, he always questions everything, wanting to reveal within the chaos of artifice the pure form of a naked breast or the reality of a gesture. The poet is a "liar" because words rarely satisfy him. They creep into a classical disorder too distant or too close to his desire. Yet, he sometimes finds the right word, the untainted speech that puts everything in its place: the landscape, the dream, or reason itself. He's then justified and returns to his precise purpose, which is to name things, to tell the truth, to open the floodgates of joy upon the great sun. Clear and simple ambitions, apparently!

But those who seek them take on simultaneously "a kingdom where the impossible is king." "I want the moon," said Caligula. Folly? Innocence? He knows that once the moon is in his hands, the impossible at last on earth, everything will be transformed, "men will never die then and will be happy." He feels ready for every party, for happiness in life. Generous promise! Before getting there, there's blood, despair, death, and the resignation of the "wise." This conquering of the moon, this insistence on the absolute, this excessive quest for happiness, the poet undertakes it. In the middle of combat, Rieux the doctor meets Grand the stylist: both struggle against the plague.

But there's more. In order to express his hope for a better world, freed from constraint and despair, Camus uses a poetic prose worthy of our greatest lyrical writers. A novelist and a philosopher, he wants to *speak* honestly, *speak* only to diagnose and to find a cure. Nevertheless, he sometimes sings, sometimes wakes up like his Stranger, "stars upon his face," feeling "the wonderful peace of the sleeping summer flow into him like a tide." The feel for images and song, the regular rhythm of the heart, the lyrical breath of the hymn, the unfettered cry that tears up the throat and rises the sun with the pride of *Chantecler*, it's all there. The nightingale and the lark are watching over. Camus is caught in his own trap. "Soon the roads on the sea will be covered with mimosa. Women will be dressed in light cloth. A vast, bright and beating sky!" Caligula exalts with clairvoyance. And Rieux, in *The Plague*, Meursault the Stranger. Despite his fear of "inhuman lyricism," his constant concern for verbal asceticism, Camus often gives his heroes a poetic language, since it is true that "his hatred for poetry is equaled only by his inability to formulate his discovery of the absurd in a form other than poetic," and this according to Pierre Desgraupes.

In Camus, as in all the restless, there's a moment when the tension subsides, when the heart overcomes the mind, and there's time for "distraction." The philosopher lets himself go, he forgets to split hairs. He goes naked into the water and smiles at the sun. He sings, he's a poet. His "hunger for clarity" is satisfied with flowers, with sand, with a warm body. The power of words ends where the freedom of joy begins. He's now "reconciled." The "unreasonable silence of the world" gives way to the bountiful echo of roads leading to the ocean and to voluptuous lips.

"It is also said that Sisyphus, nearing death, foolishly wanted to test his wife's love. He ordered her to cast his unburied body into the middle of the public square. Sisyphus woke up in the underworld. And there, irritated with an obedience that was so contrary to human love, he obtained from Pluto permission to return to earth in order to punish his wife. But upon seeing once again the face of this world, tasting the water and the sun, the warm stones and the sea, he no longer wanted to go back to the infernal darkness. Reminders, tantrums, warnings were to no avail. Many years more he lived facing the curve of the gulf, the sparkling sea, and the smiles of the earth. A decree of the gods was necessary. Mercury came and seized the audacious man by the collar and, snatching him from his joys, led him forcibly back to the underworld, where his rock was ready for him."* Camus is of those who joyfully rolls the rock. He imagines a happy Sisyphus. "One doesn't discover the absurd without wanting to write a manual for happiness. Happiness and the absurd are two sons of the same earth. They are inseparable."† This is a change from "nausea" and other shades of "vine black." This tonic and sun-filled literature, which shows trust in man, announces the solemnities of Easter following Gethsemane!

Born in this country of light that gives without measure, raised among men who yearn for pleasure, for love, for a life spent in endless nuptials with the world, Camus was well suited for singing the difficult hope and the terrible joy that allow us to survive the deadly contradiction in which we live. The Algerians don't write poems; they are themselves a luminous summer poem. When

---

* Translation taken from Albert Camus, *The Myth of Sisyphus*, translated by Justin O'Brien in *The Myth of Sisyphus and Other Essays*, Vintage (May 7, 1991).

† Ibid. It seems that Sénac left out a sentence from the original. After "One doesn't discover the absurd without wanting to write a manual of happiness," Camus writes, "'What!—by such narrow ways—?' There is but one world, however."

Camus let himself go and followed their games and their loves, he became a poet. Enthusiastic and alert, he wrote pages of singular beauty, especially in *Nuptials*. He thought of his work in terms of sun, of ocean, of love, of fraternal understanding. On the ruins of the plague, he built a generous city where we find the faces of our ancient gods, that glory which leads us some evenings to the shore, naked, free, innocent, and in pursuit of happiness.

[*direct transcription of announcer's off-voice*]

Charles Evin just read for you
A study by Jean Sénac on "Albert Camus, poet of the 'joie de vivre'"
Now to listen to poetic passages taken from *The Stranger*, *The Misunderstanding*, *Nuptials*, *State of Siege*, and *The Minotaur*.
Charles Mallet, Clément Bairam, Elyane Gautier, and Catherine Georges will lend their voices to these songs of light.

[*Follow with a reading of the chosen texts, along with the presentation of each actor's voice.*]

You have just heard poetic texts by Albert Camus, preceded by a presentation of the poet of the "joie de vivre," by Jean Sénac.
These texts taken from *The Stranger*, *The Misunderstanding*, *Nuptials*, *State of Siege*, and *The Minotaur* were read by Charles Mallet, Clément Bairam, Elyane Gautier and Catherine Georges.
The presentation was read by Charles Evin.
This show was directed and produced by Jean Sénac.
Next Monday, October 31st at 8:30 p.m., you can to listen to "Philosophy of the absurd and morality of happiness: Albert Camus," a show by Fanny Landi-Benos produced by Louis Foucher.

Literary magazine: Panel discussion on *L'Été* by Albert Camus, an interview moderated by Jean Sénac, with Edmond Brua, El Boudali Safir and Sauveur Galliéro.

(*Wednesday April 14th at 9:40 p.m.*)

Sénac: In France's literary production over the past few weeks, a particular essay has caught our attention. It's *L'Été* by our fellow countryman Albert Camus. This work, which comes 15 years after *Nuptials*, brings together texts written between 1939 and 1953. With a precision that doesn't forgo lyricism, Camus seeks to identify some of his fundamental themes: justice and beauty, and from there to define or to deepen a solar humanism in the Mediterranean tradition. In that sense *L'Été*, which emphasized the stance taken in *The Rebel* and the two volumes of *Actuelles* [*Algerian Chronicles*], can be viewed as an experimental book. We've asked our friends, the writers Edmond Brua and El Boudali Safir and the painter Sauveur Galliéro, to give us their perspective on that book and to help us establish its reach. Edmond Brua, what are your thoughts?

Brua: *L'Été* is a remarkable book in thought and style, but I would mostly like to speak about the particular moment it seems to epitomize in Camus's thought and about the significance I find in that moment. We have become too used to the idea, whether shaped by ourselves, by others, or by itself over time, that Camus is a philosopher of nonsense, of the absurd and a prophet of despair. In this book, Camus returns to his roots, i.e., the Mediterranean, Algeria, and the light, that source of all life from which everything can begin again.

Sénac: Is that your opinion, El Boudali Safir?

Safir: Yes, there's indeed in that return to the native roots of light, of sun and warmth, symbolized by the summer, a secret but pressing call for hope and for life, a life capable of overcoming its worries, its anxieties, its negations. Camus's nostalgia places him again in his true climate, the Mediterranean made of measure and equilibrium, celebrated by Audisio with less authority one should say. That climate is as far removed from the storms of despair as it is from the wild bursts of joy. One finds the same equilibrium in Muslim poets, among those most desperate, such as Abou Laâla and Chabbi,[1] who are able to preserve the spark of hope, and of faith, wise and serene.

Sénac: Sauveur Galliéro, as a painter, do you believe in this technical role of light?

Galliéro: For sure the temptation to re-create actual light, the continuity for the artist . . . can even push him to suicide.

Sénac: You're thinking of Van Gogh . . .

Galliéro: Certainly we are dealing with a Nordic subject in the presence of light. To go back to what El Boudali Safir was saying, I don't think it's possible for a Mediterranean mind.

Sénac: That's in fact Camus's position, who in his work never opted for suicide. Maybe it's because he carries in himself "an invincible summer."[2]

Brua: In the title itself, *L'Été*, there's a sort of double meaning that becomes one: first of all, the solstice, the season, then the word "été [was]" past participle of the verb "être [to be]": that which is no more, which was consumed, but that can be reborn from its ashes. This idea of a rebirth that is always possible is profoundly present in Camus, and even though it doesn't take the shape of a mystical, sentimental, or carnal hope, it expects everything from the character, even rebellion.

Safir: All rebirth is possible only if it's wanted, desired, courageously created. The will, the character, as you said, the acute awareness of the destiny of his fellow men, are crucial in this case to man, the rebel and the fighter. All of Camus's work is crafted under the dual sign of this rebellion and of this redeeming struggle.

Didn't he say so himself in *L'Été*? "If it's then true that salvation is in my hands, I will answer yes to the century's calling, because of that vigilant force and the enlightened courage that I always sense in a few men that I know."[3]

Safir: Galliéro?

Galliéro: To me, there's simply a notion of equilibrium there. If I just look at the shape of the word, there's a suggestion of equilibrium in "Été," the T as the beam between the é, the two sides of the scale.

Sénac: Yes . . . yes . . . It's funny and yet true. Basically we keep going back to the famous Mediterranean measure, which swings back and forth.

Safir: "Alternation," Montherlant would say.

Sénac: It's betwixt and between, which is in fact the title of Camus's first book.

Brua: Alternation . . . Yes. Why not dualism? I can't give a lot of quotes, but how can you forget this cry in the face of light: "Where's the world's absurdity? Is it that splendor or the memory of its absence? With so much sun in my memory, how could I have bet on nonsense."[4] We could speak of palinody, of contradiction, whereas Camus continues to question himself and to question the world. He who sees only the answer will be eternally double. Faced with that enigma, dualism is the only honest attitude that remains for the mind. "Everything is double," said Balzac, "even virtue."

Galliéro: I don't think it can be otherwise in this land of extremes and of intensity, where light consumes everything and where the brightness of day permeates even our night.

Safir: The healthy effect of this climate and invigorating light was already celebrated by Gide. It gave him back the passion and the pleasure of life, praised as a true resurrection. Pierre Louÿs, as for him, celebrates it as the actual source of poetry. In the preface for *Chansons de Bilitis*, written in Constantine, he says: "Poetry is a flower of the East that doesn't live in our warm greenhouses . . . You always have to look for it at the source of the sun . . ."

Sénac: That last book by Camus underscores nevertheless a certain attraction to solitude, and like a desire to distance one's self from the world. Camus writes in *The Minotaur*: "In order to understand the world, you sometimes need to turn away from it in order to better serve men, to hold them at a distance for a while." And later on he insists, in *La Mer au plus près*, with an almost cruel irony: "I don't have enough of all my art to hide my despair or dress it up fashionably."

Brua: Careful! Careful! Jean Sénac, I don't think that Camus is tempted by solitude, any more than he is by nonsense.

Sénac: Of course, it's an *inhabited solitude*[5] . . .

Brua: One should talk about isolation instead, which isn't the same thing. Every true artist needs human presence, but he also needs silence and the serenity that he won't find in a crowd. Here, Camus says so himself at the end of *L'Énigme*: "Yes, all that noise . . . when peace is to love and to create in silence." One mustn't look for absolute pessimism, or renunciation, or asceticism in Camus.

Sénac: Perhaps that's what he means in these sentences: "Never again will we be loners" and "So much temptation, though, at certain hours, to turn away from this dreary and emaciated world! But we live in these times and we can't live hating ourselves."[6]

Safir: Besides, it's what he says: "There's beauty and there are the humiliated,"[7] which denotes, I think, a double temptation: the isolation of the artist and the struggling rebellion of man. With all the necessary caution and reserve, one could think of the Romantics, who Camus seems to join here through an acute consciousness of his mission among men.

Galliéro: Romanticism, if by that one means the entirely natural desire of the artist to be integrated. In the end it's what creates his tragedy, or perhaps more his actions, and his works—unless he's an aesthete.

Sénac: If you don't mind, we're going to discuss a more "anecdotal" side of Camus. He's been criticized for his humor—and maybe a certain fierceness—regarding Algeria. Some have found his texts on Oran and the "cities without a past"[8] unfair.

Brua: I would simply respond that he who loves well, chastises well.

Safir: I was going to say that he mainly saw what he calls cities without a past through the eyes of a Frenchman steeped in classical culture. What tragic meaning would he have gotten, for example, had he thought of it, from the grandiose end of Tachfin, the last Almoravid, rolling off the cliffs of Santa Cruz into the harbor of Mers El Kébir! North Africa's past is full of these remarkable destinies. It's a history of men of action, more than contemplation. From Jugurtha to Abdelkader, including Abdelmoumen, Ibn Toumert, so much to think about. The thinkers themselves were committed thinkers. See Saint Augustine defending Hippone, and Ibn Khaldoun, whose life was so rich and adventurous . . . And Camus himself.

Sénac: One also notices the importance of this militant life in search of a solution, away from nihilism after it has been analyzed, in the following crucial statement, "I rebel, therefore we are."[9]

Brua: I find that message of Camus clearer than ever, within reach of the men he loves so much. And when he says: "I knew that in one night, [a single, cold and pure February night] the almonds trees of the Vallée des Consuls would be covered in flowers";[10] it's that knowledge, that certainty, which miraculously contains all the secrets of nature and of man, all the possibilities of rebirth that we search for in the dark.

Sénac: Yes, it's what the poet René Char meant when he recently wrote to me that "Poetry and man have everything to gain here. Camus properly sets fire to the ruins, while he carves out the first stones for the reconstruction."[11]

Notes

FOREWORD

1. Afifa Bererhi, who authored the most recent and most informed synthesis of these cultural and literary meetings, considered them "the most remarkable event of the colonial period in Algeria." The meetings took place at the Educational Center of Sidi Madani, near Blida, and gathered writers and artists from France, European Algerians, and "indigenous" Algerians. See her article "1948—Les rencontres de Sidi Madani: Projet culturel et enjeux politiques," in *Défis démocratiques et affirmations nationales* (Algérie, 1900–1962, ouvr. Coll. Alger, Chihab éd., 2016), 64–84.
2. Republished in Jean Sénac: *Pour une terre possible* (Paris: Marsa éd., 1999), 15–24.
3. On the editorial beginnings of *Poèmes*, see our introduction to Jean Sénac: *L'Enfant fruitier* (Algiers, El Kalima, coll. PIM, 2018).
4. Named after a series of attacks that occurred in Algeria on All Saints' Day, on November 1, 1954.

PREFACE BY THE TRANSLATOR

1. Kai Krienke, ed., *Jean Sénac: The Sun under the Weapons: Correspondence and Notes from Algeria* (*Parts 1 & 2*), *Lost & Found* (New York: CUNY The Graduate Center, 2015).

2. Among them were Beat and African American poets such as Allen Ginsberg, Gregory Corso, Lawrence Ferlinghetti, Bob Kaufman, Phillis Wheatley, George Moses Horton, Paul Laurence Dunbar, Langston Hughes, and LeRoi Jones/Amiri Baraka.

3. Frantz Fanon, The Wretched of the Earth (New York: Grove Press, 2007), 31.

4. In fact, according to Hamid Nacer-Khodja, on September 24, 1956, Fanon handed to Sénac the letter of resignation he had written to minister Lacoste, which was to be published in the review *Exigence* along with Sénac's manifesto *The Sun under the Weapons*. This was on the eve of Fanon's departure for Tunis, two days after the First Congress of Black Artists and Writers, held in Paris from September 19 to 22.

5. A detailed account of Sénac's close connection with Subervie can be found in Hamid Nacer-Khodja's essay "Un editeur en guerre d'Algérie: Jean Subervie," http://www.revues-plurielles.org/_uploads/pdf/4_41_2.pdf.

INTRODUCTION

1. Herbert R. Lottman, *Albert Camus* (Paris: Seuil, 1978) [*Albert Camus: A Biography* (Gingko Press, 1996)] and Olivier Todd, *Albert Camus: Une vie* (Paris: Gallimard, 1996, collection "Vies" [*Albert Camus: A Life* (Da Capo Press, 2000)]. Émile Temime and Nicole Tuccelli, *Jean Sénac l'Algérien, le poète des deux rives* [Jean Sénac the Algerian, poet of the two shores] (Paris: Autrement, collection "Littératures," 2003).

2. Authors who have briefly commented on the Sénac-Camus relationship.

3. From the Sénac collections at the Bibliothèque de l'Alcazar (Fonds Littéraires méditerranéens), Marseille, and at the Bibliothèque nationale d'Algérie, Algiers. Sénac generally kept copies of the letters he sent, as well as those he received. The excerpts of the correspondence between Sénac and Camus, as well as those from the journals and other cited manuscripts of Sénac are from the first collection, unless otherwise mentioned.

4. According to Rabah Belamri in *Jean Sénac: Entre désir et douleur* [Jean Sénac: Between desire and pain] (Algiers: OPU, collection "Classiques maghrébins," 1989), 7.

5. Sénac's texts, where he states that his entire life was in his writing, are too numerous

and varied to be cited individually. The following personal statement should suffice: "There is no separation between my poetry and myself, I am alive within my literature . . . I have committed everything to it." *Journal Alger* (janvier–juillet 1954) [Algiers Journal, January–July 1954] (Pézenas: Le Haut Quartier, collection "Méditerranée vivante," 1983), 39.

6. Albert Camus, *Carnets I* (Paris: Gallimard, collection "Blanche," 1962), 69 [*Notebooks 1935–1942*, ed. Ivan R. Dee (Tra Rep, 2010)].

7. Albert Camus, *Carnets II* (Paris: Gallimard, collection "Blanche," 1964), 24 [*Notebooks 1942–1951*, ed. Ivan R. Dee (Tra Rep, 2010)].

8. Jean de Maisonseul (Algiers, August 3, 1912–Cuers, June 3, 1999), painter and urban architect, disciple of Le Corbusier. Friend of Camus's, who included him in the call for civil truce and then took part in his release from prison. He knew all of the major writers and artists who lived in Algeria from 1930 to 1976, the year he settled in Cuers (Var), France. A great friend of Algeria, after its independence, he worked as curator at the National Museum of Fine Arts (Musée national des Beaux-arts) (1962–1970) and as director at the Institute for Urbanism of the University of Algiers (1970–1975). He was a part of the Jean Sénac Literary Committee as established in Sénac's will. He contributed greatly to the poet's posthumous fame, and had been his loyal companion from 1946 to 1973.

CHAPTER 1. BIRTH OF A FRIENDSHIP

1. Sénac began his literary career by publishing his poems in the *Bulletin des jeunes* (The youth newsletter) (Vichy, November 1942) and most importantly in the weekly magazine *Le Pique-Boeuf* (Rabat, starting in February 1944).

2. As stated by Sénac in his article "Notes sur le roman algérien [Notes on the Algerian novel]," in *Orphys*, Paris, no. 2 (October 1947): 152–163. Also see his statement to Jean-Pierre Péroncel-Hugoz, in *L'Afrique littéraire et artistique* [Artistic and literary Africa], Paris, no. 15 (February 1971): 20–24 (reprinted in *Poésie au Sud: Jean Sénac et la nouvelle poésie algérienne d'expression française* [Poetry in the South: Jean Sénac and the new Algerian poetry of French expression] (Marseille: Archives of City of Marseille, 1983), 26–28; and Jean-Pierre Péroncel-Hugoz, *Assassinat d'un poète* [Assassination of a poet] (Marseille: Quai-Jeanne Laffitte, 1983), 33–36.

3. These were the "Santa Cruz" poems, dated August 19, 1946, in *Afrique*, Algiers, no.

211 (September/October 1946), and "Mesure d'homme [Measure of man]," dated October 1946 in *Vent Debout*, Koblenz, no. 1948. [Translator's note: *Vent Debout* was a literary review created by René Wintzen in the aftermath of WWII that featured unpublished texts by French and German writers.]

4. Mainly in "Notes sur la jeune poésie algérienne [Notes on the new Algerian poetry]," in *Méditerranée* (Meknès), no. 28, September 1946 (Republished in "Jean Sénac," *Journal Alger*, 111–116, *Poésie au Sud*, 45–46, and *Orphys*, 152–163).

5. An immense activity that we will have to give justice to one day.

6. *Paris* (Casablanca), no. 208 from July 8, 1947.

7. *Orphys*, 163.

8. On "Alger, capitale des lettres françaises en exil [Algiers, capital of French letters in exile]," refer to *Vie culturelle à Alger, 1900–1950* [Cultural life in Algiers, 1900–1950] (edited by Paul Siblot) (Montpellier: Praxiling-University Paul Valéry-Montpellier III, 1996).

9. On the Lélian circle, see Jean Déjeux, "Jean Sénac à Alger: Le Cercle Lélian, 1946–1949 [Jean Sénac in Algiers: The Lélian Circle, 1946–1949]," in *AWAL*, "Spécial Jean Sénac," Paris, no. 10 (1993): 93–104.

10. The friendship between Sauveur Galliéro, the anti-conformist painter (Algiers 1914–Paris 1963), and Camus dates back to before the war. Aside from inspiring in part the character of Meursault—we will come back to that later—Camus helped Galliéro financially when he was living in Oran (from January 1941 to August 1942) and also prefaced one of his shows in Paris in 1945. Sénac acknowledged many times his own indebtedness toward an artist to whom he owed "almost everything" (preface to Sauveur Galliéro's retrospective at the French Cultural Center of Algiers from May 25 to June 10, 1967, *Visages d'Algérie: Regards sur l'art* [Faces of Algeria: Views on art] (Paris: Méditerranée, EDIF, 2000, 2002), 193.

11. In *Afrique*, Algiers, no. 212 (November–December 1946).

12. Letter dated 1947 (National Library of Algeria, Algiers, Sénac Collection).

13. Camus belonged to Gallimard's reading committee; there he directed the collection "Espoir" starting in 1945 (first title appearing in 1946).

14. Blanche Balain, *Temps lointain* [Distant time], preface by Albert Camus (Paris: Charlot, 1946). Sénac cited excerpts from this collection in his letter, in Jean Sénac, *Pour une terre possible*, 209–210.

15. *Journal de sana* [Sanatorium journal], July 7, 1947, unpublished (National Library of

Algiers, Algiers, Sénac Collection).

16. *AWAL*, no. 10 (1993): 186. Republished in Blanche Balain, *Mémoire* (Antibes: La Tour des Vents Pierre-François Astor, 1998).

17. Reproduced in Jean-Pierre Péroncel-Hugoz's work *Assassinat d'un poète*, 125–126.

18. On June 10, according to H. Lottman, *Albert Camus* (Paris: Éditions du Seuil, 1978), 436, and Roger Grenier, *Albert Camus: Soleil et ombre* [Albert Camus: Sun and shadow] (Paris: Gallimard, collection "Blanche," 1968), 109.

19. Albert Camus, *Essais* (Paris: Gallimard, Bibliothèque de la Pléiade, 1965), 99.

20. Jean Sénac, *Avant-Corps* [Forebody] (Paris: Gallimard, collection "Blanche," 1968), 109.

21. For Camus, see Abdallah Naaman's *La Mort et Camus* [Camus and death] (Sherbrooke: Naaman, 1980). Sénac, aside from the recurrent theme of death in his work, had written his testament seven times (according to Jacques Miel, his adopted son), the last one dating from May 2, 1973 (reproduced in *Le Soleil fraternel: Jean Sénac et la nouvelle poésie algérienne d'expression française* (Marseille: Quai-Jeanne Laffitte, 1985), 35–36. Finally, we notice that thirteen years separate the births and deaths of both Camus (1913–1960) and Sénac (1926–1973).

22. "Christian anarchist" was an expression that Emmanuel Roblès used when referring to Sénac, mentioned by the latter in a letter dating June 16, 1947, in *Pour une terre possible*, 210.

23. This feature had notably been studied by Jean Onimus in *Camus* (Paris: Desclée de Brouwer, collection "Les Écrivains devant Dieu [Writers facing God]," no. 2, 1965); R. P. Jacques Goldstein, "Camus et la Bible [Camus and the Bible]," *La Revue des lettres modernes*, "spécial Albert Camus," 4 (Paris, nos. 264–270, 1971), 97–140; Ruth Reichelberg, *Albert Camus: Une approche du sacré* [Albert Camus: A view of the sacred] (Paris: Nizet, 1983). See also Camus's statement in *Carnets III* [*Notebooks, Volume 3*] (Paris: Gallimard, collection "Blanche," 1987), 128: "I do not believe in God and I'm not an atheist." Was it one of those literary formulas that "strike but don't enlighten"? (*Carnets III*, 51).

24. Sénac, *Avant-Corps*, 58.

25. According to Roger Quilliot, in Albert Camus, *Essais*, 1916.

26. Paris.

27. Camus was born in Mondovi (Dréan, today), a city that is situated 25 km south of Annaba (previously Bône). Rivoli, now Hassi-Mamèche, is 17 km southeast of

Mostaganem. Fabrication is a way of being and of action in the works of the poet (used three pseudonyms, language ruses such as borrowing without citing, citations truncated or out of context, textual variations, neologisms, etc.).

28. Albert Camus, *Carnets II* [*Notebooks, Volume 2*], 81 and 201.

29. Sénac kept the majority of the articles on Camus published between 1946 and 1952 (National Library of Algeria, Algiers, Sénac Collection).

30. "Visages d'Algérie: Albert Camus [Faces of Algeria: Albert Camus]," in *Oran Républicain* [newspaper of Oran], September 30, 1947.

31. Letter from June 30, 1947 (National Library of Algeria, Algiers, Sénac Collection).

32. Interview given to *Alger Soir*, November 15, 1947.

33. The manuscript of this show is held at the National Library of Algeria, Algiers, Sénac Collection. The novel *The Plague* would be adapted for a movie by the Argentinian Luis Puenzo, only in 1992.

34. Sénac does mention difficulties of daily life in his *Journal de sana*.

35. Albert Camus, *Journaux de voyage* [published in English as *American Journals*] (Paris: Gallimard, collection "Blanche," 1978).

36. The *Journal de sana* [Sanatorium journal] was kept from January 17, 1947, to January 13, 1948.

37. Jean Déjeux, "Les Rencontres de Sidi-Madani (Algérie) [The Sidi-Madani meetings (Algeria)]," *Revue de l'Occident musulman et de la Méditerranée* [Review of the Muslim West and of the Mediterranean], Aix-en-Provence, no. 20 (second semester, 1975): 165–174.

38. *M* [review], Algiers, no. 1 (March 1949).

39. *Poésie au Sud*, 66.

40. This collection brings together poetry that was published for the most part in *Afrique* (Algiers), in issues no. 209 of May–June 194[5] to no. 223 of May–June 1948.

41. Camus, *Essais*, 69.

42. Ibid.

43. In *M*, 5–6.

44. H. Lottman, *Albert Camus*, 467, mentions that Camus "met with Roblès, Brua and other old acquaintances."

45. Concerning Sénac and the radio, see our presentation "La critique radiophonique de Jean Sénac: Essai de présentation analytique [Jean Sénac's radio critique: Analytical presentation essay]," in *Les Écrivains et la radio* [Writers and the radio], international

colloquium May 23–25, 2002 (directed by Pierre-Marie Héron) (Montpellier: University of Montpellier III–Center for 20th Century Studies, 2003).

46. National Library of Algeria, Algiers, Sénac Collection.

47. Manuscript drafted on September 17, 1948 (National Library of Algeria, Algiers, Sénac Collection).

48. On *Empédocle*, see Albert Camus–Jean Grenier, *Correspondances* (Paris: Gallimard, collection "Blanche," 1981), 262; Roger Grenier, *Albert Camus: Soleil et ombre* [Albert Camus: Sun and shadow], 198; René Char, Œuvres complètes [Complete works] (Paris: Gallimard, Bibliothèque de la Pléiade, 1983), 77.

49. Two texts, "Le verbe désincarné [The disembodied word]" and "Miroir de l'églantier" [Mirror of the wild rose], are published in *Empédocle*, Paris, no. 9 (March–April 1950). They are included in *Poèmes* (Paris: Gallimard, collection "Espoir," 1954).

50. First letter from Char to Sénac, dated November 13, 1949 (Alcazar Library of Marseille, Sénac Collection).

51. Second letter from Char to Sénac, dated April 19, 1950 (Alcazar Library of Marseille, Sénac Collection).

52. See Jean Déjeux, "La revue algérienne *Soleil* (1950–1952) fondée par Jean Sénac et les revues culturelles en Algérie de 1937 à 1962 [*Soleil* review (1950–1952), founded by Jean Sénac and the cultural reviews of Algeria from 1937 to 1962]," in *Présence francophone*, Sherbrooke, no. 19 (Fall 1979): 5–28, and *Alger Républicain*, August 2, 1950.

53. No. 83, July 1954.

54. On Edmond Charlot, see Michel Puche, *Edmond Charlot éditeur* (Pézénas: Domens, 1995), and the compilation by F.-J. Temple, *Alger au temps des "Vraies Richesses"* [Algiers in the era of "Vraies Richesses"] (Loess: Pont-de-Salars, no. 13, 1984).

55. Correspondence of Jean Sénac and Sauveur Galliéro in 1950, National Library of Algeria, Algiers, Sénac Collection.

56. *Alger Républicain*, August 2, 1950, is the only media outlet that announced the news, while *La Dépêche quotidienne d'Alger* interviewed the poet on August 28, 1950.

57. Title of an article by Sénac, in *Oran Républicain*, January 21, 1947.

58. With the notable exception of René Char, "Maître constant [Constant master]," in Jean-Pierre Péroncel-Hugoz, *L'Afrique littéraire et artistique*, or "Maître intact [Untouched master]," in Jean Sénac, *Dérisions et vertige* [Derisions and vertigo] (Arles: Actes Sud, 1983), 21.

CHAPTER 2. ALGERIANISM OR ÉCOLE D'ALGER

1. See the letter from Jean Sénac to Jean Daniel, *Poésie au Sud*, 66.
2. Sénac contributed mostly to *L'Africain*—no. 636 from July 3, 1946, to no. 685 from June 2, 1947—with twenty-two literary and artistic reviews, and to *Oran Républicain*—from December 26, 1946, to April 6, 1948—giving them articles and poems signed "Jean Sénac," but also "Gérard Comma," or "L'Eschotier d'Alger [The chronicler of Algiers]."
3. *La Dépêche quotidienne d'Alger*, August 3, 1950.
4. See note 40 from the previous chapter.
5. The passages on Robert Randau and Algerianism come from the following sources (in chronological order of publication):
   - *Revue algérienne des sciences juridiques, économiques et politiques* [Algerian review of judicial, economic, and political sciences], special edition of *Roman colonial et idéologie coloniale en Algérie* [Colonial novel and colonial ideology in Algeria], Algiers, no. 1 (March 1974).
   - Jean Déjeux, "Robert Randau et son 'Peuple franco-berber' [Robert Randau and his 'Franco-Berber people']," in *Cahiers de Littérature générale et comparée*, special edition of *Littérature coloniale*, Paris, no. 5 (Fall 1981): 91–99.
   - Alain Calmes, *Le Roman colonial en Algérie avant 1914* [The colonial novel in Algeria before 1914] (Paris: L'Harmattan, 1984).
   - Paul Siblot, "Pères spirituels et mythes fondateurs de l'algérianisme: Le roman colonial 1 [Spiritual fathers and the founding myths of Algerianism: The colonial novel 1]," *Itinéraires et Contacts de cultures*, vol. 7 (Paris: L'Harmattan, 1987).
   - Jean Déjeux, "Robert Randau, théoricien du Roman colonial: Le roman colonial 2 [Robert Randau, theorist of the colonial novel: The colonial novel 2]," *Itinéraires et Contacts de cultures*, vol. 12 (Paris: L'Harmattan, 1990).
   - Paul Siblot, "L'Algérianisme: Fonction et dysfonction d'une littérature coloniale: Le roman colonial 2 [Algerianism: Function and dysfunction of a colonial literature]," *Itinéraires et Contacts de cultures*, vol. 12 (Paris: L'Harmattan, 1990).
6. Jean Sénac, *Le Soleil sous les armes* [*The Sun under the Weapons*] (Rodez: Subervie editions, 1957), 35.
7. Jean Sénac, Ébauche du père [Sketch of the father], 109.
8. *Oran Républicain*, January 28, 1947. Reprinted in Jean Sénac, *Pour une terre possible* [For a possible land], 283–284.

9. This was Camus's statement to Gaétan Picon, in *Le Figaro Littéraire*, Paris, August 10, 1946.

10. Jean Sénac, "Littérature engagée? Le roman algérien [Committed literature? The Algerian novel]," in *L'Africain*, Algiers, no. 636 (July 8, 1946).

11. *L'Africain*, Algiers, no. 686 (June 9, 1947).

12. *Soleil*, Algiers, no. 1, January 1950; no. 7–8, February 1952 (last issue). Intended as a trimestral review, its publication was irregular. The number of pages varied from 45 to 140 and circulation was between 750 and 2000 copies.

13. Jean Sénac, *Pour une terre possible*, 285.

14. National Library of Algeria, Algiers, Sénac Collection.

15. PPA [Parti du Peuple Algérien/Party of the Algerian People], founded on March 11, 1937, in Algiers by Messali Hadj (1898–1974), considered the "father" of Algerian nationalism. It was banned, then reconstituted on October 20, 1946, as the MTLD [Mouvement pour le Triomphe des Libertés Démocratiques/Movement for the Triumph of Democratic Freedoms] with the same charismatic leader. It was ultimately dissolved on November 3, 1954, after the start of the Algerian War on November 1, 1954.

    UDMA [Union Démocratique du Manifeste Algérien/Democratic Union of the Algerian Manifesto], moderate nationalist party advocating for integration, created in Algiers in March 1946 by Ferhat Abbas (1899–1985).

    PCA [Parti Communiste Algérien/Algerian Communist Party]. It "officially" separated from the French Communist Party on October 17 and 18, 1954.

16. "Lettre d'un jeune poète algérien [Letter from a young Algerian poet]," in Jean Sénac, *Pour une terre possible*, 241.

17. Ibid.

18. "Décadence et grandeur de Camus" is the title of an article that was going to be published in the second issue of *M*, which we weren't able to find . . . if it was even written.

19. This is how Gabriel Audisio referred to him in "L'Algérien," in *Hommage à Albert Camus* (Paris: Gallimard, 1967), 40.

CHAPTER 3. THE SON FACES THE FATHER

1. Jean Sénac, *Avant-Corps* [Forebody], 113.

2. Testimony of Jean de Maisonseul (1999).

3. As Char had called him, on the back of a postcard he sent to Sénac on October 15, 1950 (Alcazar Library of Marseille, Sénac Collection).

4. On Sénac's theater, see the essays by Rabah Bélamri, in *Levant*, Paris, no. 3 (1990): 20–28, and in *AWAL*, no. 10 (1993): 51–59.

5. The French branch of Vineta editions (Switzerland) was located 19, rue du Vieux Colombier, Paris V.

6. This "preface" was included as a "foreword" to the *Poèmes* collection. Char reused certain terms and took out two concluding expressions, the adverbs "courageously" and "authentically."

7. Was included in Jean Sénac, *Pour une terre possible*.

8. Letter from Sénac to Char, Paris, October 4, 1950 (Alcazar Library of Marseille, Sénac Collection). Michèle Ombla is in reality Michèle Lévi-Provençal, half-sister of Nicole Galliéro, Sauveur Galliéro's wife.

9. Jean-Pierre Péroncel-Hugoz, *L'Afrique littéraire et artistique*, 21, and *Le Monde*, September 13, 1973, included in *Assassinat d'un poète*, 44–46 and in *Poésie au sud*, 115–117. Jean Sénac, *Ébauche du père*, 72.

10. Jean Sénac, *Ébauche du père*, 72.

11. He stayed there until December 1951. Twice, by mistake, Camus wrote "Hostel for Beekeeping Apprentices [Foyer des apprentis apicoles]" on the envelopes of his letters.

12. On the lack of real time dedicated to friends, see Camus, *Carnets III* [*Notebooks, volume 3*], 76.

13. October 18, 1951, according to H. Lottman, *Albert Camus*, 505; November 2, 1951, according to O. Todd, *Albert Camus: Une vie*, 556.

14. *Soleil*, Algiers, no. 5 (February 15, 1951): 13–21.

15. Albert Camus–Jean Grenier, *Correspondance*, 78.

16. *La Table Ronde*, Paris, January 1948; *Empédocle*, Paris, April 1949; *Cahiers du Sud*, Marseille, January 1951.

17. Albert Camus, *Essais*, 438–443.

18. Ibid., 407–709.

19. H. Lottman, *Albert Camus*, 501.

20. Camus's article "Lautréamont et la banalité," taken from *L'Homme révolté*, published in *Cahiers du Sud*, infuriated André Breton, who responded in several articles for

Arts.

21. Sénac responds to André Breton's writings, "Sucre Jaune," in *Arts*, Paris, no. 328 (October 11, 1951); "Dialogue entre André Breton et Aimé Patri," in *Arts*, no. 333 (November 16, 1951); and "Lettre à *Arts*," no. 335 (November 30, 1951). National Library of Algeria, Algiers, Sénac Collection.

22. See Jean Sénac's "Critique de l'existentialisme," in *Méditerranée*, Meknès, no. 16 (June 15, 1946), and *Visages d'Algérie: Regards sur l'art*, 217–219, concerning his meeting with Simone de Beauvoir.

23. Jean Sénac, *Pour une terre possible*, 214–215.

24. Jean Sénac, *Journal Alger*, 19.

25. *Le Soleil noir/Positions*, Paris, no. 1 (February 1952): 90–93. The questions asked by the review were (1) Is the condition of the rebel justified? (2) What is for you the meaning of rebellion in today's world?

26. These citations correspond to pages 704 and 707, in *Essais.*

27. Postcard from Jean Grenier to Jean Sénac (Alcazar Library of Marseille, Sénac Collection).

28. Jean Sénac, *Le Soleil sous les armes*, 55. The Camusian influences in Jean Sénac's work still need to be established.

29. In addition to the controversy started by *The Rebel*, Camus's mother had broken her leg and was to undergo a surgical operation.

30. Albert Camus, *Carnets III*, 15.

31. Jean Sénac, *Poèmes* (Arles: Actes-Sud, 1986), 135 (republished with variations, notes, and poems by the author).

32. Concerning the habits of Gallimard's review committee, see O. Todd, *Albert Camus: Une vie*, 513–515.

33. "*NRA: Nouvelle Revue Algérienne* [New Algerian Review]," proposed title for *Terrasses.*

34. Albert Camus, *Carnets III*, 273.

35. See in particular Loess, Pont-de-Salars, nos. 18–19, 1985, special issue, *La Terre et la Fertilité* [Earth and fertility]—*Albert Camus.*

36. In *L'Exil et le royaume* [*Exile and the Kingdom*], Albert Camus, "Théâtre, Récits, Nouvelles" (Paris: Gallimard, Bibliothèque de la Pléiade, 1962), 1559–1575.

37. With Sénac as director, the editorial committee included Maurice-Robert Bataille, Mohamed Dib, Sauveur Galliéro, Jacques Lévy, Jean de Maisonseul, Mouloud

Mammeri, Jean-Pierre Millecam, Louis Nallard, Aïcha Nekoud, José Pivin, and Jean Rime. The manifesto's signatories, aside from the director and the members of the editorial committee, were Albert Camus, Kateb Yacine, and Mouloud Feraoun.

38. Jean Sénac, *Pour une terre possible*, 286.

39. Jean Sénac, Ébauche du père, 72.

40. The issue featuring Camus's preface wasn't published until 1959 (see Camus, *Essais*, 163; and 1959, René Char, Œuvres complètes [Complete Works], lxxx and 1293.)

41. Radio program "Un compagnon dans la nuit [A companion in the night]: René Char" (manuscript of the program *Poésie sur tous les fronts* [Poetry on all fronts], from September 1, 1967, in Jean Sénac, *Pour une terre possible*, which reproduced parts of Camus's text).

42. *La Pensée de midi*, Marseille, no. 1 (Spring 2000): 191–197.

43. Consecutively in *Le Soleil noir/Positions*, 90–93; "Merci à René Char," in *L'Action*, Tunis, December 30, 1957; the radio program "Un compagnon dans la nuit: René Char," op. cit.

44. Albert Camus, *Essais*, 867–876.

45. There are minor variations: three in punctuation (in the excerpt of *Medea*, for example) and five in style, more concise than in the original version. Another strange detail, the essay is dated 1952 in *Terrasses* and 1953 in the edition of *L'Été* where it was included (incorporated into *Essais*). According to the correspondence he received from Camus, Sénac should have known that it was written in 1953.

46. There's no mention of it in the edition of *Essais*. Regarding a picture of the covers of *Terrasses* and *Simoun* contained in the Albert Camus photo album (Paris: Gallimard, La Pléiade, 1982), 213, Jean Grenier points out "Camus's participation in Algerian reviews." Rabah Bélamri, in much the same vein, mentioned only that *Terrasses* published a text by Camus, in his introductory note for the anthology Écrivains francophones du Maghreb [Francophone writers of the Maghreb] (edited by Albert Memmi) (Paris: Seghers, 1985), 316. No reference was made to Camus's text in *Littérature et temps colonial* (edited by Jean-Robert Henry and Lucienne Martini) (Aix-en-Provence: Edisud, 1999), 341–342, despite a photograph of the cover of *Terrasses*, considered to be "an exceptional representation of fraternity in Algeria and the Mediterranean." Only the catalog for the show on Albert Camus at the University of Nice, May 8–14, 1980 (Aix-en-Provence: Edisud, 1981), 65, underlines that "Retour à Tipasa" was published in *Terrasses*, without mentioning nevertheless

that it was the original version.

47. The *Nouvelle NRF* [*Nouvelle Revue Française*], Paris, July 1953 (article not signed), and September 1953 (note from René Etiemble in his comprehensive article "Barbarie ou Berbérie [Barbary or Berbery]"); *Les Cahiers du Sud*, Marseille, no. 318, 1st semester 1953 (article by Jean Ballard).

48. Paris, PUF, 1952.

CHAPTER 4. TOWARDS A POLITICAL LITERATURE

1. See "Alger de l'aube" [Algiers of the dawn], in *Terrasses*, no. 1, 123–124, republished in *Poésie au Sud*, 48.

2. "Lettre d'un jeune poète algérien" [Letter of a young Algerian poet] (Paris: November 1950) and "Les Assassins en Algérie [The assassins in Algeria]," in Jean Sénac, *Pour une terre possible*, 241–244.

3. See Sénac's letter to Jean Daniel, *Poésie au Sud*, 66.

4. Those names were mentioned by Jean-Pierre Péroncel-Hugoz, in *L'Afrique littéraire et artistique*.

5. Aside from hiding a clandestine press, his cellar (near the Admiralty neighborhood) was also the meeting place for most of the nationalist leaders and of the "liberal French" (testimony by Jean de Maisonseul, 1999).

6. After March 1940—when he settled in Paris, following the decision to suspend *Soir Républicain* in January 1940—Camus only saw a handful of urban Arab intellectuals. This doesn't mean, of course, that he didn't stand up for some of the "Arabs" (and Kabyles), in his writings and interventions, and this until the end of his life.

7. "La Patrie [The Homeland]," in *Matinale de mon peuple* [Dawn of my people] (Rodez: Subervie, 1961), 47.

8. See his letter to Jean Daniel, *Poésie du Sud*, 67.

9. The series was published in *Simoun*, Oran, no. 8 (April 1953) (seven poems). After 1954 they were included in other journals and republished as a separate, revised, and enriched collection in *Matinale de mon people*.

10. *Consciences algériennes*, no. 1, December 1950.

11. Title of an Algerianist novel by Ferdinand Duchêne, *Les Barbaresques: Au pas lent des caravanes* (Paris: Albin Michel, 1922).

12. Albert Camus, *Essais*, 504.

13. *Le Monde*, Paris, July 19–20, 1953.

14. See in particular, in chronological order, the works of Jean-Pierre Péroncel-Hugoz; Jean Déjeux, *Littérature maghrébine de langue française* (Sherbrooke: Naaman, 1973) and *Jean Sénac vivant* (Paris: Saint-Germain-des-Prés, collection "Les Cahiers de Poésie 1," no. 4, 1981); Rabah Bélamri, *Jean Sénac, entre désir et douleur* (Algiers: OPU, 1989).

15. See Sénac's letter to Jean Daniel, in *Poésie au Sud*, 67–68.

16. Albert Camus, *Essais*, 1840.

17. Jean Sénac, *Journal Alger*, 20, 24, 30, 44, 61, and 71.

18. Ibid., 18–19.

19. See "Misère de la Kabylie [Misery in Kabylia]" and "Crise en Algérie [Crisis in Algeria]," in Albert Camus, *Actuelles III: Chroniques Algériennes, Essais*, 903–959. [Translated in *Algerian Chronicles*, Belknap Press/Harvard University Press.]

20. Jean Sénac, *Journal Alger*, 44 [49 in 1996 edition].

21. Ibid., 71 [76 in 1996 edition].

22. Ibid., 73 [79 in 1996 edition].

23. Ibid., 65–66 [71 in 1996 edition].

24. See, for example, Abdelhamid Ben Badis's (1899–1940) famous statements on "Arabo-Islamism." He was one of the founders, in 1932, of the Association of Muslim Algerian Ulemas ("reformist scholars") (Law on association of July 1, 1901), considered to be one of the main ideologues of post-independence Algeria: "Islam is our religion, Arabic our language, Algeria our homeland." "The Algerian people are Muslim and connected to the Arab identity."

25. Jean Pomier, *Chroniques d'Alger (1910–1957) ou le temps des Algérianistes* (Paris: La Pensée Universelle, 1972), and H. Lottman, *Albert Camus* (Paris, Éditions du Seuil, 1978), 544–545.

26. H. Lottman, *Albert Camus*, 445.

27. At the beginning of spring 1954, according to H. Lottman, *Albert Camus*, 545; in January 1954, according to O. Todd, *Albert Camus: Une vie* (Paris: Gallimard, collection "Biographie," 1996), 814.

28. Jean Sénac, *Journal Alger*, 38 [42 in 1996 edition].

29. Signed manuscript with autograph, National Library of Algeria, Algiers, Sénac Collection.

30. Jean Sénac, *Matinale de mon peuple*, 47–49.

31. Albert Camus, *Carnets III*, 109.

32. Jean Sénac, *Journal Alger*, 90. Later on, in his answer to a Proust questionnaire, Sénac states that Dien-Bien-Phu was "the military action that I admire the most," in Jean-Pierre Péroncel-Hugoz, *Assassinat d'un poète*, 39. Regarding Casablanca, the poet mentions the bloody repression on December 7 and 8, 1952, after Mohamed V (1909–1961) reaffirmed his determination to be independent.

33. Jean Sénac, *Journal Alger*, 61.

34. Ibid., 64–65.

35. Jean-Pierre Péroncel-Hugoz, *L'Afrique littéraire et artistique*. Sénac—under the pseudonym Gérard Comma, his mother's maiden name—had already highlighted the "Algerian consciousness" in the same novel by Mammeri, in *Terrasses*, 95.

36. He notes 50,000 on May 17, 1954, in *Journal Alger*, 49.

37. Jean Sénac, *Les Désordres* (Paris: Saint-Germain-des-Prés, 1972), republished in Déjeux, *Jean Sénac vivant*.

38. "Oran ou les statues sous la peau" was first published in *Simoun*, Oran, no. 21 (1956): 64–69, then in a different version in *Poésie au Sud*, 57–60.

39. Albert Camus, *Essais*, 809–832.

40. Jean Sénac, "Littérature engagée? Le roman algérien," in *L'Africain*, Algiers, no. 641, August 21, 1946.

41. Typed manuscript, National Library of Algeria, Algiers, Sénac Collection.

42. Alcazar Library of Marseille, Sénac Collection.

43. *Poésie au Sud*, 118. André Bélamchi is the editor (and main translator) of Federico Garcia Lorca's Œuvres complètes [Complete works], Bibliothèque de la Pléiade (Paris: Gallimard, 1984).

44. An advance payment of 40,000 (letter from Gaston Gallimard to Sénac, on July 30, 1954; Alzacar Library of Marseille, Sénac Collection). Louis Daniel Hirch, known for being the press's inescapable sales director, writes to Sénac the same day to clarify that "with regard to the advance, this was discussed between Michel Gallimard and Camus" (Municipal Library of Marseille, Sénac Collection).

CHAPTER 5. NOVEMBER 1954: THE "JUST" FIGHT OR TERRORISM?

1. Poem dated April 1955. Reworked and completed under the title "Ébauche du père [Sketch of the father]," in *Les Désordres*, 99–105.

2. Albert Camus, *Essais*, 1606 and 1814.

3. Camus only met with Spanish Republicans who were exiled in France, whereas Sénac came across Republicans who were exiled within Spain, during his two visits there (July 12 to August 18, 1958, and July 2 to October 8, 1959). He met with several poets there, including Blas de Otero, who shared the same democratic ideal (parallel struggle against Francoism, on one hand, and colonialism on the other) and the same aesthetic concerns (Otero's "social poetry" intersects with Sénac's militant poetry). The *Diwân espagnol* [Spanish Diwan], written during his second stay, confirms these affinities. See Jean Déjeux, "Le Diwân espagnol de Jean Sénac," in *Espagne et Algérie au XXème siècle: Contacts culturels et création littéraire* [Spain and Algeria during the 20th century: Cultural contacts and literary creations], ed. J. Déjeux and P. H. Pageaux (Paris: L'Harmattan, collection "Récifs," 1985), 179–187.

4. "Littérature engagée? Le roman algérien [Militant literature? The Algerian novel]," *L'Africain*, Algiers, no. 643, August 21, 1946.

5. Jules Roy, *Mémoires barbares* (Paris: Albin Michel, 1989), 373.

6. Admissions like this are often found in Sénac's correspondence and unpublished writings. In published pieces, see for example Ébauche du père, 72, and *Poésie au Sud*, 65.

7. In his *Carnet* [Notebook] dated October 4, 1954 (Alcazar Library of Marseille, Sénac Collection), Sénac specifies that the proposal was to "begin as program editor at Radio Alger and to direct the literary show. Minimum salary: 65,000 francs."

8. The quotes from *Carnet 1954* are found in Jean Sénac, *Pour une terre possible*, 246. The review was published in the *Times Literary Supplement* dated November 5, 1954. For reference, 1,532 copies of the *Poèmes* collection were sold by June 30, 1959. Some 812 copies were destroyed and 300 were given to the author (letter from Gallimard to Sénac on October 9, 1959, Alcazar Library of Marseille, Sénac Collection).

9. See Jean Daniel's letter in *Poésie au Sud*, 67. Sénac had been corresponding with François Mauriac since June 1953. The latter had promised an article for *Terrasses* (letter to Sénac, October 7, 1953), Alcazar Library of Marseille, Sénac Collection).

10. Albert Camus, *Carnets III* [*Notebooks, volume 3*], 29.

11. Jean Sénac, *Pour une terre possible*, 245–248.

12. See his articles published in *Combat* from May 1945, titled "Crise en Algérie [Crisis in Algeria]," in *Actuelles III: Chroniques algériennes, 1939–1958*, 939–959.

13. Jean Grenier, *Albert Camus: Souvenirs* (Paris: Gallimard, collection "Blanche," 1968),

11.

14. Letter from Suzanne Agnely to Jean Sénac dated November 24, 1954 (Alcazar Library of Marseille, Sénac Collection).

15. Jean Sénac, *Poèmes*. In his unpublished collections from that period—*Fortifications pour vivre* [Fortifications to live] (1950–1952) and *Atelier du soleil* [The workshop of the sun] (1954) (republished in Jean Sénac, *Pour une terre possible*)—Sénac repeatedly admits that poets lie, adopting Nietzsche's line "But poets lie too much," in *Thus Spoke Zarathustra*.

16. See for example his response in *Journal Alger*, 45, to a Muslim journalist from *La République algérienne* who described the entire collection of poems as "insincere." Thus began the relationship of Sénac the Algerian, who defied his community of origin in order to join another that already distrusted him.

17. Jean Sénac's friend Jean Todrani, a poet from Marseille, witnessed the birth of the famous signature. See his testimony in *AWAL*, no.10 (1993): 129.

18. These well-known figures eventually became ministers in independent Algeria, with multiple portfolios.

19. Jean Sénac, *Pour une terre possible*, 189–190. French troops, 5,000 soldiers—a number mentioned in his poem—began their first military operations under the code name "Véronique," during January 18–24.

20. See Mohamed Harbi's testimony in *Une Vie debout: Mémoires politiques, 1945–1962* [A life upright: Political memoirs, 1945–1962], vol. 1 (Algiers: Casbah, 2001), 193.

21. According to H. Lottman, *Albert Camus* (Paris: Editions du Seuil, 1978), 541, *L'Écho d'Alger* was already a staunch supporter of French Algeria.

22. Jean Sénac, *Pour une terre possible*, 248.

23. See his articles in *Combat*, in Albert Camus, *Essais*, 954–958.

24. Jean Sénac, "Les intellectuels algériens et la revolution [Algerian intellectuals and the revolution]," in *Poésie au Sud*, 68; also see his letter to Jean Daniel, ibid., 67.

25. Benjamin Stora and Zakya Daoud, *Ferhat Abbas* (Paris: Denoël, 1995, and Algiers: Casbah ed., 1995).

26. O. Todd, *Albert Camus: Une vie* (Paris: Gallimard, collection "Biographie," 1996), 613–618.

27. Jean Sénac, *Carnet 1955* (Alcazar Library of Marseille, Sénac Collection). Also see André Bélamchi's testimony in *Poésie au Sud*, 118.

28. *Esprit*, Paris, no.10–11 (November 1955): 1675–1680.

29. Letter from Suzanne Agnely to Sénac dated October 12, 1955 (Alcazar Library of Marseille, Sénac Collection).

30. Similar to the two mentioned previously (see note no. 18), these two figures would occupy important ministerial and state positions in independent Algeria. Rédha Malek would even be head of state (prime minister) from August 21, 1993, to April 11, 1994.

31. Ahmed Taleb-Ibrahimi, *Lettres de prison* [Letters from prison] (Algiers: SNED, 1966 and 1977), 40, and *De la colonization à la revolution culturelle* [From colonization to the cultural revolution] (Algiers: SNED, 1973), 182.

32. Interview in *La Guerre d'Algérie*, by Patrick Eveno and Jean Planchais (Paris: La Découverte-Le Monde, 1989, and Algiers: Laphomic, 1990), 182.

33. O. Todd, *Albert Camus*, 723.

34. See *El Moudjahid*, the so-called Yugoslavian edition (printed in Yugoslavia), 1962, 3 vols., 1: 3.

35. Account given by Jean de Maisonseul (interview with the author on July 5, 1997, and letter of October 2, 1997).

36. National Library of Algeria, Algiers, Sénac Collection. The afterword is dated "Pointe-Pescade, May 1966–April 1967." It was partially published—specifically these excerpts collected by Guy Dugas—in *Algérie, un rêve de fraternité* [Algeria, a dream of fraternity] (Paris: Omnibus, 1997), 854, and entirely published in Jean Sénac, *Pour une terre possible*, 300–305.

37. *France Observateur*, Paris, no. 279, September 1955. See Robert Barrat, *Les Maquis de la liberté: Un journaliste au coeur de la guerre d'Algérie* [The hills of freedom: A journalist at the heart of the Algerian War] (Paris-Algiers: Témoignage Chrétien-Entreprise Algérienne de Presse, 1992).

38. Short of money, Sénac sold the manuscript of *Poèmes* to the bookstore Les Argonautes (coffee-table books and autographs) located at 74, rue de Seine, Paris VI, on October 5, 1955. A year earlier, on October 13, 1954, he sold a copy of the first edition of *L'Envers et l'endroit* [Upside down, right side up] (Algiers: Charlot, 1937) signed "to Jean Sénac, in memory of home, Albert Camus," for 10,000 francs.

39. "I don't say anything about what I think," Albert Camus, *Carnets III*, 252.

40. Jean Sénac, *Ébauche du père*, 72. The nickname "resolute Scipion" appears in Camus's autograph for Sénac in *The Misunderstanding and Caligula*, 3rd ed. (Paris: Gallimard, collection "Blanche," 1949).

CHAPTER 6. THE CIVIL TRUCE

1. Albert Camus, *Essais*, 983–988.

2. *Esprit*, Paris, March 1956, 335–339. This text, included in a report titled "Négocier en Algérie [Negotiating in Algeria]," was republished in *Poésie au Sud*, 60–63, and partially republished in *Algérie, un rêve de fraternité* [Algeria, a dream of fraternity], 849–852.

3. See Charles Robert Ageron, "L'évolution de l'opinion publique française face à la guerre d'Algérie [The evolution of French public opinion during the Algerian War]," in *Revue d'Études Historiques*, Université d'Alger (Institut d'Histoire), no. 9 (1993): 1–15.

4. See *Alger Républicain* from November 22, 1938, on Edmond Brua's *Les Fables bônoises* [Fables from Bône], also published by Algiers: Carbonel, 1938; Algiers-Paris: Charlot, 1946; Paris: Balland, 1972.

5. Jean Sénac, "Un Français d'Algérie prend la parole: Assez de massacres! [A French Algerian speaks: Enough massacres!]," in Jean Sénac, *Pour une terre possible*, 249–252.

6. Albert Camus, *Essais*, 992.

7. Jean Sénac, "Un Français d'Algérie prend la parole."

8. Albert Camus, *Essais*, 355.

9. Jean-Jacques Brochier, *Camus, philosophe pour classes terminales* [Camus, a philosopher for senior year classes] (Paris: Balland, 1979), 66.

10. Jean Sénac, "Un Français d'Algérie prend la parole." Also see his letter to Robert Llorens, in *Poésie au Sud*, 40.

11. Jean Sénac, ibid.

12. Albert Camus, *Essais*, 993.

13. Ibid., 1872–1877.

14. Guy Dugas, "Albert Camus et l'épisode de la Trêve civile [Albert Camus and the Civil Truce episode]," *Guerre d'Algérie* magazine, Saint-Cloud, no. 6 (November–December 2002): 40–45.

15. Amar Ouzegane, *Le Meilleur Combat* (Paris: Julliard, 1962), 235.

16. Le Cercle du Progrès, with cheikh El Okbi as one of its founding presidents, defended by Camus in *Alger Républicain* in 1939, was located at 9, place du Gouvernement (Place des Martyrs today). It was the headquarters of the Association of Muslim Algerian Ulemas.

17. The "Zone Autonome d'Alger" was a military subdivision that was part of Wilaya 4 (Algiers) during the Algerian War. Zones and *wilayas* (of which there were six) are sections of Algeria recognized by the Congress of Soummam on August 20, 1956.

18. Jean Sénac, *Œuvres poétiques* (Arles: Actes Sud, 1999), 387.

19. Amar Ouzegane, *Le Meilleur Combat*.

20. The inscription was in Amar Ouzegane's copy, ibid., deposited at the National Library of Algeria, Algiers, Sénac Collection.

21. National Library of Algeria, Algiers, Sénac Collection.

22. See *Poésie au Sud*, 41.

23. Ibid., 41 and 68.

24. Jean Sénac, "Un Français d'Algérie prend la parole." Jean de Maisonseul confirmed that Guy Mollet had received him and his "liberal" and "Arab democrat" friends on the evening of the "Day of the Tomatoes"—addressing them in campaign rhetoric—while Robert Lacoste had refused to see them and had his secretary answer between closed doors that he "didn't want to fight simultaneously against the liberals and the *fellaghas*" (Personal letter belonging to the author, March 23, 1999).

25. Jean Sénac, "Un Français d'Algérie prend la parole."

26. Albert Camus, *Essais*, 99.

27. Jean Sénac, "Un Français d'Algérie prend la parole."

28. Albert Camus, *Essais*, 995.

29. Camus gives the following reasons for his departure, to his friend André Rosfelder: "I left *L'Express*, almost immediately, for two apparently contradictory reasons, which nevertheless define my position: Mauriac's adherence to France-USSR and Mollet's exhibition in Algiers," in *Marseille*, review of the city of Marseille, no. 120 (1st trimester 1980): 105–109.

30. *Les Cahiers du Sud*, Marseille, no. 334 (April 1956): 414–415. Republished in *Les Désordres*. These poems are "Vieillesse" (p. 17), "La Confusion" (p. 29), "Le poème" (p. 42), and "La Vanité" (pp. 54–55).

31. In May 1956 according to H. Lottman, *Albert Camus* (Paris: Editions du Seuil, 1978), 554; more specifically, on May 16, 1956, according to O. Todd, *Albert Camus: Une vie* (Paris: Gallimard, collection "Biographie," 1996), 637.

32. Camus, *Essais*, 1001–1008.

33. Ibid.; Letter from Jean de Maisonseul to the author, March 23, 1999.

34. Jean Sénac, *Le Soleil sous les armes*.

35. The collection *Diwân de l'État-Major* would be partially included in *Matinale de mon peuple*.

36. Jean Sénac, "Kateb Yacine et la littérature nord-africaine," *L'Action*, Tunis, July 30, 1957; *Perspectives ouvrières*, Paris, no. 89, September 19, 1956; *Entretiens sur les Lettres et les Arts*, Rodez, February 1957.

37. Sénac, "Kateb Yacine et la littérature nord-africaine."

38. Jean Sénac, *Pour une terre possible*, 301.

39. Interview with the author, 1999.

40. Jean Sénac, *Pour une terre possible*, 199–192.

41. Jean Sénac, *Avant-Corps*.

42. See Camus's acknowledgment, in *Carnets II* [*Notebooks, volume 2*], 317: "My entire work is ironic."

43. *Carnet 1962*, National Library of Algeria, Algiers, Sénac Collection.

44. *Présence Africaine*, Paris, nos. 8–10 (1956): 380–381. Sénac inserted the poem in *Matinale de mon peuple*, without mentioning Kateb Yacine and Henri Kréa. Sénac had known the publication's directors (notably Mario de Andrade) since January 1956.

45. *Poésie au Sud*, 65.

46. H. Lottman, *Albert Camus*, 599.

47. "Camus raciste? [Camus, a racist?]" (Jean Cassin) in *La Revue des lettres modernes*, Albert Camus series, no. 5 (1972): 275–278 (Paris: Minard, 1973). It is a review of Conor Cruise O'Brien's book *Albert Camus* (Paris: Seghers, collection "Les Maîtres Modernes," 1970).

48. Jean Grenier, *Albert Camus: Souvenirs*, 171.

49. Albert Camus, *Essais*, 988.

50. Alcazar Library of Marseille, Sénac Collection [now located at the Bibliothèque de l'Alcazar, Marseille].

51. Albert Camus, *Essais*, 322.

52. Excerpts quoted by Jean Sénac in *Ébauche du père*, 72. They correspond to act 4, scene 1, and are incorrectly transcribed. The original text is as follows: To Chaerea's question "Are you then with him?," the young Scipion answers, "No. But I cannot be against him." Then, two lines later, when Chaerea bitterly remarks, "He denies what you are confessing. He mocks what you worship," Scipion answers, "It's true, Chaerea. But there's something in me that's similar to him. The same flame burns

our hearts." Albert Camus, *Théâtre, récits, nouvelles* (Paris: Gallimard [Bibliothèque de la Pléiade], 1962), 85.

53. Albert Camus, *Théâtre, récits, nouvelles*, 84.

54. Jean Sénac, *Ébauche du père*, 72.

CHAPTER 7. FROM A LITERATURE OF COMBAT TO THE NOBEL PRIZE

1. *Exigence*, no. 5 (January 1956): 26–46 (3, place des Vosges, Paris IV).

2. It would be included in Frantz Fanon's posthumous work, *Pour la Révolution africaine* [*Toward the African Revolution*] (Paris: Maspéro, 1964).

3. *Exigence*, 45. Sénac refers to this piece by Camus, which appears in his article "La justice, elle aussi, a ses pharisiens [Justice also has its pharisees]," in *Caliban*, Paris, no. 39 (May 1950): 24. The writer did not include it in *Actuelles II* (1953), but it was later added to *Essais*, 1725.

4. Olivier Todd, *Albert Camus: Une vie* (Paris: Gallimard, 1996), 674. Camus's name appears in the "press service" list that Sénac created (Alcazar Library of Marseille, Sénac Collection).

5. Albert Camus, *Essais*, 1843, and *Réflexions sur le terrorisme* [Reflections on terrorism] (edited by Jacqueline Lévi-Valensi) (Paris: Nicolas Philippe, 2002), 173–176.

6. The references are as follows: Roger Quilliot, *La Mer et les prisons: Essai sur Albert Camus* [The sea and the prisons: Essay on Albert Camus] (Paris: Gallimard, collection "Les Essais," 1980 [revised and corrected edition]), 299; H. Lottman, *Albert Camus* (Paris: Editions du Seuil, 1978), 601, and O. Todd, *Albert Camus: Une vie*, 674–675; Albert Camus, *Réflexions sur le terrorisme*, 173–176.

7. Autographed rough copy, National Library of Algeria, Algiers, Sénac Collection.

8. Conor Cruise O'Brien, *Albert Camus* (Paris: Seghers, collection "Les Maîtres Modernes," 1970), 88.

9. Emmanuel Mounier, *Malraux, Camus, Sartre, Bernanos* (Paris: Seuil, 1953).

10. Olivier Todd, *Albert Camus: Une vie*, 707. The minute of the correspondence is deposited at the National Library of Algeria, Algiers, Sénac Collection.

11. This statement was confirmed by Jacques Miel (1999).

12. Text cited by Olivier Todd, *Albert Camus: Une vie*, 675.

13. Afterword to the reprint of *Soleil sous les armes*, in Jean Sénac, *Pour une terre possible*, 301.

14. Ibid., 300.

15. Alcazar Library of Marseille, Sénac Collection.

16. *Libération*, Paris, March 6, 1958.

17. *Les Lettres françaises*, Paris, no. 714, March 20–26, 1958.

18. The letter is signed by Claude Gallimard (Alcazar Library of Marseille, Sénac Collection).

19. Alcazar Library of Marseille, Sénac Collection.

20. *Poésie au Sud*, 41.

21. The picture is published in *Poésie au Sud*, 47, and the autograph can be found in Jean-Pierre Péroncel-Hugoz's book, *Assassinat d'un poète*, 27.

22. Jean-Pierre Péroncel-Hugoz, *Assassinat d'un poète*, 27.

23. In the following two texts: "Lettre d'un jeune poète algérien [Letter from a young Algerian poet]" and "Les assassins en Algérie [The assassins in Algeria]," in Jean Sénac, *Pour une terre possible*, 241–244.

24. Jean Sénac, "La Patrie," in *Matinale de mon peuple* [Dawn of my people], 48.

25. Albert Camus, *Essais*, 1606 and 1814.

26. Ibid. See also *Carnets II*, 290 ("Le désespéré n'a pas de patrie [The hopeless have no country]") and 337 ("J'ai une patrie, la langue française [I have a country, the French language]").

27. See in particular Laurent Mailhot, *Albert Camus ou l'imagination du desert* [Albert Camus or the imagination of the desert] (Montréal: University of Montreal Press, 1973), 121–140, and *Camus et la politique* (edited by Jeanyves Guérin) (Paris: L'Harmattan, collection "Histoire et Perspectives Méditerranéennes," 1986), 196–197.

28. Jean Daniel, *Le Temps qui reste* (Paris: Stock, 1973), 99.

29. Jean Daniel, cited by Jules Roy, in *Camus* (Paris: Hachette, collection "Génies et Réalités," 1964), 205; and O. Todd, *Albert Camus: Une vie*, 620–621.

30. Albert Camus, *Essais*, 875.

31. Albert Camus, *Carnets III*, 214.

32. Ibid., 216.

33. Ibid., 222.

34. Ibid., 250.

35. Ibid., 251.

36. Albert Camus–Jean Grenier, *Correspondance*, 222.

37. Albert Camus, *Essais* (see in particular the foreword and "Algérie 1958").

38. *Demain*, Paris, October 24–30, 1957 (in Albert Camus, *Essais*, 1902–1903); *La Revue prolétarienne*, Paris, no. 121, November 1959; *Le Monde*, Paris, December 14, 1957 (Albert Camus, *Essais*, 1881–1882).

39. *Poésie au Sud*, 69–72. All of Sénac's citations are taken from this article, unless stated otherwise.

40. Olivier Todd, who consulted the Camus collection at the Institut Mémoires de l'Édition Contemporaine [Institute for Contemporary Publishing Archives] (IMEC) in Paris, cites a few excerpts in his book, *Albert Camus: Une vie*, 707. As for the letter of transmission that accompanied Sénac's article to Camus, an autographed minute was deposited at the National Library of Algeria, Algiers, Sénac Collection.

41. See Sénac's letter to Llorens, *Poésie au Sud*, 42. As for Camus's response to Sénac, it was deposited at the National Library of Algeria, Algiers, Sénac Collection.

42. Ibid.

43. [Translation of slang word "louette"] *Louette*: Sly, clever, in *pied-noir* Algerian slang. See André Lanly, *Les Français d'Afrique du Nord: Étude linguistique* (Paris: Bordas, collection "*Études supérieures*," 1970), 97–98; Roland Bacri, *Trésors des racines pataouètes* (Paris: Berlin, collection "Le français retrouvé," 1983), 110.

44. Republished in *Algérie, un rêve de fraternité*, 59–154.

45. Malek Haddad, "Les zéros tournent en rond," essay, preceded by *Écoute et je t'appelle*, poems (Paris: Maspéro, 1961), 32.

46. Jean Sénac, *Le Soleil sous les armes*, 20.

47. Jean Sénac, *Journal d'Alger*, 44.

48. Ibid., 29.

49. The letter to Jean-Michel Guirao was mentioned in his *Carnet 1960* (National Library of Algeria, Algiers, Sénac Collection). The special issue was titled "Camus l'Algérien," *Simoun*, Oran, no. 32, 9 (1960). Concerning this expression "Camus Algérien [Algerian Camus]," which Gabriel Audisio used for the first time in an article with the same title (*Algéria*, Algiers, no. 1 [October 1948]: 37–38), see Laurent Mailhot's excellent synthesis in *Albert Camus ou l'imagination du désert*, 125 n. 12.

50. See Sénac's letter to Jean Daniel, in *Poésie au Sud*, 65.

51. *Ophrys.*

52. *Méditerranée.*

53. In the short story "L'Hôte [The Guest]" in *L'Exil et le royaume* [*Exile and the Kingdom*], *Essais*, 1609–1623, literary fiction seems to match Camus's vision of the

future of Algeria at war. A short summary will provide argumentation along these lines. Daru, a teacher in the high plateaus of Algeria, received from an old friend and policeman (Balducci) the assignment to hand over a criminal, an Arab (anonymous) who had killed his cousin (the prisoner was tied to the saddle of the horse with a rope). After having given him shelter and food, Daru leads his one-night-only "close enemy"—almost reluctantly and by moral humanism—to the intersection of the paths that lead either to "the administration and the police" or toward the nomadic tribes where he could be reunited with his "people." The Arab man heads for the first path. Upon his return, Daru notices threats against him on the classroom's blackboard, and becomes a "solitary" man but not yet a man of "solidarity" (terms that we see in "Jonas ou l'artiste au travail [Jonas, or the Artist at Work]" in the same collection), words that translate rather explicitly Camus's private and public position on Algeria: not denying his communitarian identity, nor approving of violence. It's hard to imagine, in this highly symbolic story, that an Arab man would choose France and its justice in order to prevail—on top of having committed an ordinary crime—while his colleagues are in rebellion against France ("there could soon be a rebellion"), at least again its colonial system. For Camus—as mentioned before—the justice applied to "Arabs" must be under France's control. This short story can't be appreciated without considering a political motive since, as Roger Quilliot points out, the manuscript (dated July 1954) was not only significantly modified for its reprint in March 1957, but "one would need, in order to fully understand 'The Guest' to refer to *Actuelles III: Chroniques algériennes* [*Algerian Chronicles*]," in *Théâtre, Récits, Nouvelles*, 2049.

54. Unpublished draft of an unsent letter from Sénac to Camus, dated November 15, 1956.

55. Tayeb Bouguerra, *Le Dit et le non-dit: À propos de l'Algérie et des Algériens chez Camus* [The told and the untold: Concerning Algeria and Algerians in Camus's work] (Algiers: OPU-ENAL, n.d. [1991]), 168.

56. See *La Guerre d'Algérie* (edited by Henri Alleg), vol. 2 (Paris: Temps Actuels, 1981), 564–565, and O. Todd, *Albert Camus: Une vie*, 684–685, as well as Camus, *Carnets III*, 177. Bensaddok became General Secretary of the JFLN (Jeunesse du Front de Libération Nationale [National Liberation Front Youth]) after Algeria's independence in 1962.

57. See his statement in *Théâtre, Récits, Nouvelles*, 1717.

58. Albert Camus, "Lettres à un ami allemand [Letters to a German friend]," in *Essais*, 241.

59. Cited by Madeleine Bouchez, *Les Justes—Camus* (Paris: Hatier, collection "Profil d'une œuvre," 1974), 19.

60. Albert Camus, *Essais*, 1845.

61. Ibid., 1882–1883.

62. Benjamin Stora, *Histoire de la guerre d'Algérie* (Paris: La Découverte, collection "Repères," 1995), 28, and *La Gangrène et l'oubli: La mémoire de la guerre d'Algérie* [Gangrene and oblivion: Memory of the Algerian War] (Paris: La Découverte, collection "Essais," 1998), 25–28.

63. Albert Camus, *Essais*, 1882.

64. Rodez: Subervie, 1960, 203.

65. Albert Camus, *Actuelles III*, in *Essais*, 1013.

66. See, for example, the essay by Christiane Achour-Chaulet, "Albert Camus, Alger: 'L'Étranger' et autres récits" (Biarritz: Atlantica, collection "Les colonnes d'Hercule," 1998, the chapter "Un retour à Camus?" in particular, 180–197).

67. Preface by Tayeb Bouguerra, in *La Peste* (Algiers: ENAG, collection "El Aniss," 1995).

68. Jean-Pierre Péroncel-Hugoz, *Assassinat d'un poète*, 29.

69. *Poésie du Sud*, 41.

70. Djamel Amrani, "Le plein chant d'un cœur blessé [The full chant of a wounded heart]," in *AWAL*, no. 10 (1993): 155.

71. Herbert Lottman, *Albert Camus*, 633.

72. Interview with Jean de Maisonseul from July 5, 1997, and letters from him to the author dated October 2, 1997, and March 23, 1999.

73. National Library of Algeria, Algiers, Sénac Collection.

74. Olivier Todd, *Albert Camus: Une vie*, 352.

75. Albert Camus, *Essais*, 352.

76. National Library of Algeria, Algiers, Sénac Collection.

77. *AWAL*, no. 10 (1993): 12–24.

78. Jean Sénac, *Pour une terre possible*, for example pages 149 and 244.

79. "Au Pont des Arts," 6, rue Bonaparte in Paris V. The show lasted until May 24, 1958. Albert Camus prefaced the catalog.

80. Ibid. Letter from Jean de Maisonseul dated March 23, 1999.

81. This article was published in *L'Action*, Tunis, May 12, 1958 (also in Jean Sénac, *Pour*

une terre possible, 255–256).

82. Letter from Jean Sénac to Robert Llorens, *Poésie au Sud*, 42.

83. Jean Sénac, *Ébauche du père*, 72, and Sénac's last letter to Camus, dated April 29, 1958 (National Library of Algeria, Algiers, Sénac Collection).

84. According to Olivier Todd, *Albert Camus: Une vie*, 685.

85. The question of Camus's intervention and those he intervened for appears in the following works: *Essais*, 1844–1846; H. Lottman, *Albert Camus*, 605; O. Todd, *Albert Camus: Une vie*, 683–686.

86. Jean Sénac, *Ébauche du père*, 72.

87. Ibid.

88. Manuscript deposited at the National Library of Algeria, Algiers, Sénac Collection.

89. Photocopy deposited at the National Library of Algeria, Algiers, Sénac Collection.

CHAPTER 8. SÉNAC, READER OF CAMUS

1. Jean Sénac, *Pour une terre possible*, 216–225.

2. Bernard Pingaud: "There needed to be the Algerian War for the first political criticisms of *The Stranger* to appear" (Bernard Pingaud comments on *L'Étranger d'Albert Camus* [Albert Camus's *The Stranger*] [Paris: Gallimard, collection "Foliothèque," 1992], 97).

3. Albert Camus, *Carnets II*, 50.

4. Albert Camus, *Carnets I*, 202.

5. Ibid., 34. In *The Rebel*, the writer nevertheless states that "A character is never the novelist who created it," in *Essais*, 448. In *L'Été* [*Summer*], he tries to be "an objective writer," that is an author who takes on subjects without taking himself as an object, ibid., 864.

6. Jean Cathelin, "Avant *L'Étranger* [Before *The Stranger*]," Paris, *Le Nouvel Observateur*, no. 136, 21–27 (June 1967): 38. This article was cited only in *Revue des Lettres modernes*, "Albert Camus," series 2, 1968, p. 239, Minard, 1969.

7. Concerning the "absence of Arabs," it would be wrong to place a derogatory judgment upon Camus. One has to take his true thought into consideration, one of great humility, exemplified by the following two unpublished passages (personal collection).

   In reference to *The Plague*, Mouloud Feraoun wrote him the following from

Taourite-Moussa (Kabylia) on May 27, 1951: "I read *The Plague* and believe that I understood your book like I understood no other. I regretted that among all the characters there wasn't a single native and that Oran was for you just an ordinary French precinct. Oh! It isn't a criticism. I simply thought that if there weren't that divide between us, you would have known us better. You could have spoken about us with the same generosity you show toward everyone else. I still regret, with all my heart, that you don't know us enough and that we have no one to understand us, to make you understand and to help us understand ourselves." Feraoun had already mentioned this correspondence in a letter to Roblès (in *Lettres à ses amis* [Paris: Seuil, collection "Méditerranée," 1969], 54).

Camus answers from Paris on June 2, 1951: "Don't think that if I haven't mentioned the Arabs of Oran, it's because I feel separate from them. It's because in order to present them, you have to talk about the problem that poisons our everyday life in Algeria; I would've had to write a different book than the one that I wanted to write. And, besides, I'm not sure I have the talent one needs to write that other book—you could perhaps write it since you know how to effortlessly place yourself above the stupid hatreds that dishonor our country."

8. Albert Camus, *Noces*, in *Essais*, 74.
9. Alcazar Library of Marseille, Sénac Collection.
10. A handwritten testimony from journalist and writer Serge Michel (1922–1997) is deposited at the Sénac Collection of the National Library of Algeria, Algiers. He was a militant for the Algerian cause during and after the Algerian War and information manager for Casbah Films during that time. The other film producers are Dino de Laurentis, an Italian, and the Office national du Cinéma et de l'Industrie cinématographique (ONCIC).
11. *Carnets 1966–1967*, National Library of Algeria, Algiers, Sénac Collection.
12. *An Nasr*, Constantine, February 18, 1967.
13. Ahmed Taleb-Ibrahimi, *De la décolonisation à la révolte culturelle*, 161–184.
14. See Jean-Pierre Péroncel-Hugoz's testimony in *Assassinat d'un poète*, 53 and 141–149.
15. Laâdi Flici, *Albert Camus ou la crise de la littérature bourgeoise* [Albert Camus or the crisis of bourgeois literature], Algiers, éditions universitaires (1967), 19 pp. (mimeographed).
16. See his article, "Un grand écrivain français natif d'Oranie," *Paris* 228, August 8, 1947.
17. Manuscript draft, National Library of Algeria, Algiers, Sénac Collection.

18. Jean Sénac, *Pour une terre possible*, 226–237.

19. National Library of Algeria, Algiers, Sénac Collection.

20. *Les Désordres.*

21. *L'Afrique littéraire et artistique.*

22. *Le Monde Diplomatique*, Paris, August 1973, p. 22; republished in *Poésie au Sud*, 110–114.

23. See *Tous Algériens*, brochure of the GPRA (Provisional Government of the Algerian Republic), Tunis, March 1961. Sénac published three texts there: "Lettre à un jeune Français" (passages), "La Patrie" (passages) (in *Matinale de mon peuple*), "Droite et frappée dans le soleil" (in *Matinale de mon peuple*).

24. See poems "Racaille ardente" and "Cette ville," in *Dérisions et vertige*, 108–110 and 112–116.

25. Title of a poem and of a collection by Sénac (Rodez: Subervie, 1967, and Charlieu: La Bartavelle ed., 1997).

26. Title of a poem by Sénac dated August 6, 1972, in Jean Sénac, *Pour une terre possible*, 204.

CONCLUSION

1. Jean Sénac's statements on the "divine mission" of literature are abundant and consistent, particularly concerning poetry. See in particular the works of Jean Déjeux, *Jean Sénac vivant*, 252–253.

2. Jean Sénac, *Journal Alger*, 45.

3. Albert Camus, *Carnets I*, 45.

4. Albert Camus, *Carnets II*, 35.

5. Ibid., 180.

6. Albert Camus, *Carnets III*, 182.

JEAN SÉNAC AND ALBERT CAMUS'S CORRESPONDENCE

1. Claude de Fréminville (1914–1966). Writer, friend of Camus and of Sénac, he published all of his works with Charlot (Algiers and Paris) and Gallimard. Journalist for the Parisian weekly *Le Populaire*, he wrote reviews of Sénac's collections. He ceased to write in 1954, and joined *Europe 1* as an editorialist under the pseudonym Claude Terrien.

2. Poem published in *Afrique*, Algiers, no. 211 (September–October 1946): 3–4.

3. In fact these lines from *Temps lointain* (Paris: Charlot, 1946) are: "Sad in their drunkenness / Alone with their loves / Who play out their lives in broad daylight."

4. The first version of this correspondence was published in Jean Sénac, *Pour une terre possible* (Paris: Marsa, 1999), 209–210.

5. Published in *Afrique*, no. 211 (September–October 1946): 5.

6. Published in *Afrique*, no. 215 (March–April 1947): 1–2.

7. Published in Jean Pierre Péroncel-Hugoz, *Assassinat d'un poète* (Marseille: Éditions du Quai/Jeanne Laffitte, 1983), 125–126.

8. Letter published in *Poésie au Sud: Jean Sénac et la nouvelle poésie algérienne d'expression française* [Poetry in the South: Jean Sénac and the new Algerian poetry of French expression] (Marseille: Archives of the City of Marseille, 1983), 47.

9. Unpublished collection of Sénac, combining for the most part poems published in *Afrique*.

10. Sénac will publish his "Lettre ouverte à Isidore Isou [Open letter to Isidore Isou]" in his mimeographed review *M*, no. 1, March 1949.

11. Novel by René-Jean Clot, *Fantômes au soleil—Noirs de la vigne* (Paris: Gallimard, collection "Blanche," 1948).

12. This is Brice Parain, whom Sénac met at Sidi Madani.

13. Collection published in Jean Sénac, *Pour une terre possible*, 25–35.

14. *Sensibles*, series of poems combined in Jean Sénac, *Poèmes* (Paris: Gallimard, collection "Espoir," 1954).

15. Jean Vagne, editor of the review *Empédocle*, which included eleven issues: no. 1 (April 1949); no. 11 (August 1950).

16. It's *Terre possible*, partially included in *Poèmes*.

17. In Jean Sénac, *Poèmes*.

18. Text written on the back of a postcard: "Countryside of Grasse."

19. The first version of this letter was published in Jean Sénac, *Pour une terre possible*, 211–212.

20. Simone Weil, *L'Enracinement* (Paris: Gallimard, collection "Espoir," 1950).

21. Sénac wrote this text on a piece of paper, mentioning that it was written on the back of a postcard he sent to Camus.

22. Included in its entirety in Jean Sénac, *Poèmes*.

23. *NRA, Nouvelle Revue Algérienne* [New Algerian Review].

24. Baya (1931–1998), Algerian painter. Her real name being Fatima Haddad, Baya was a recognized artist (a show at Galerie Maegh, in Paris in November 1947, was prefaced by André Breton) when Sénac met her at Jean de Maisonseul's home in Algiers in 1949. The poet celebrated her in several poems and contributed to her "rediscovery" after Algeria's independence.

25. Correspondence published in *Poésie au Sud: Jean Sénac et la nouvelle poésie algérienne d'expression française*, 124.

26. Typed letter.

27. Text on the back of a postcard representing a "Panorama of Lake Geneva and the Alps."

28. Typed letter.

29. Typed correspondence with a copy of a letter Camus had sent to Jean Pomier (Toulouse, 1886–1977). Jean Pomier, a writer who lived in Algeria from 1910 to 1957, spoke Arabic and had encouraged many "Muslim" writers. President of the Association of Algerian Writers [Association des Écrivains algériens], which stemmed from the Algerianist school [Algérianisme], from 1922 to 1957, *rapporteur* of the Grand Literary Prize of Algeria [Grand Prix Littéraire de l'Algérie], and director of the review *Afrique* from 1924 to 1955, Jean Pomier helped Sénac in his early years and corresponded with him from 1946 to 1948. A literary prize and a street in his native town were named after him.

30. Léon-Gabriel Gros, editor in chief of *Cahiers du Sud*.

31. Included in Jean Sénac, *Les Désordres* (Paris: Librairie Saint-Germain-des-Prés, collection "Poètes contemporains," 1972).

32. It's called "Oran ou les statues sous la peau [Oran or the statues under the skin]," published in *Simoun*, Oran, no. 21 (1956) and *Poésie au Sud: Jean Sénac et la nouvelle poésie algérienne d'expression française*, 57–60.

33. Date stamped by the post office on the back of a postcard "Paris, the booksellers."

34. Letter published in Jean Sénac, *Pour une terre possible*, 214–215.

35. Original manuscript draft written by Sénac. With regard to the receiver, this handwritten note from Sénac: "Not sent upon the 'categorical' intervention of Yacine Kateb, who believes that we 'must *accommodate* Camus for the time being for reasons of political opportunity.'"

36. Published in Albert Camus, *Réflexions sur le terrorisme* (Paris: Nicolas Philippe, 2003), 174–176.

37. Postcard. Catherine and Jean Camus Fund. Reproduced in Olivier Todd, *Albert*

Camus: Une vie (Paris: Gallimard, collection "Biographie," 1996), 675.

38. Not selected by *L'Action* (Tunis), this article is featured in *Poésie au Sud: Jean Sénac et la nouvelle poésie algérienne d'expression française*, 67–69.

39. Collection of poems by René Char (Paris: Gallimard, collection "Espoir," 1946).

40. Partially included in Jean Sénac, *Matinale de mon peuple* (Rodez: Subervie, 1961), and published in its entirety as "Diwân du Môle," in Jean Sénac, *Pour une terre possible*, 105–146.

41. These two lines are from René Char, in *Feuillets d'Hypnos* [Leaves of Hypnos].

42. Sénac is referring to his article "Noël Favrelière" published in *Tribune du Peuple*, Paris, December 21, 1957. Deserter of the French army during the Algerian War, Noël Favrelière published a story, *Le Désert à l'aube* [The desert at dawn] (Paris: Éditions de Minuit, 1960) (republished, 2001), and *Le Déserteur* (Paris: Éditions Lattès, 1973).

43. It was impossible for us to identify this priest.

TWO SHOWS FROM RADIO ALGERIA, PRODUCED BY JEAN SÉNAC

1. Abou Ala Maâri (973–1058), an Arab poet and prose writer, and Abou'l Kacem Châbbi (1909–1934), a Tunisian poet.

2. In "Retour à Tipasa [Return to Tipasa]."

3. In "Prométhée aux enfers [Prometheus in Hell]."

4. In "L'Énigme [The Enigma]."

5. In "Le Minotaure ou la halte d'Oran [The Minotaur, or the Halt in Oran]."

6. In "L'Exil d'Hélène [Helen's Exile]."

7. In "Retour à Tipasa."

8. The exact title of the essay is "Petit Guide pour des villes sans passé [Little Guide for Cities without a Past]."

9. In *L'Homme révolté* [*The Rebel*].

10. In "Les Amandiers [The Almond Trees]." The sentence fragment in square brackets isn't in the manuscript.

11. Letter published in Jean Sénac, *Pour une terre possible*, 214–215. In fact, René Char wrote: "Poetry is safe here," and further on, "even if some details are debatable (it is to a man's honor when he risks being contradicted and admits it), *The Rebel* sets fire to the ruins, properly, while simultaneously carving out the first stones for the reconstruction."

Bibliography

T his bibliography contains only the list of works and documents cited in the text.*

Works by the Authors

Jean Sénac

WORKS

Poèmes, Paris, Gallimard, collection « Espoir », 1954. Réédition avec notes, variantes et vers de l'auteur, Arles, Actes Sud, 1986, avant-propos de René Char.

Le Soleil sous les armes, Rodez, Subervie, 1957.

Matinale de mon peuple, Rodez, Subervie, collection « Le Soleil sous les armes », 1961, préface de Mostefa Lacheraf.

Citoyens de beauté, Rodez, Subervie, 1967. Réédition (facsimilé de l'original), Charlieu, La Bartavelle ed., collection « Le Manteau du Berger », 1997.

Avant-Corps, Paris, Gallimard, collection « Blanche », 1968.

---

* All titles were left in original format, except for a few additional comments by the author that were translated.

Les Désordres, Paris, Éditions Saint-Germain-des-Prés, collection « Poètes contemporains », 1972. Réedition, in *Jean Sénac vivant*, Paris, Éditions Saint-Germain-des-Prés, collection « Les Cahiers de Poésie 1 », 1981.

Dérisions et vertige, Arles, Actes Sud, 1983, préface de Jamel-Eddine Bencheickh.

Journal Alger (janvier–juillet 1954), Pézenas, Le Haut Quartier, collection « Méditerranée Vivante », 1983. Réédition, Saint-Denis, Novelté, 1996, préface de Jean Pélegri.

Ébauche du père, Paris, Gallimard, collection « Blanche », 1989, préface de Rabah Bélamri.

Œuvres poétiques, Arles, Actes Sud, 1999, préface de René de Ceccaty, postface de Hamid Nacer-Khodja. This volume contains all of the published collections, i.e., fifteen titles.

Pour une terre possible: Poèmes et autres textes inédits, Paris, Marsa, 1999. Texts compiled, annotated, prefaced, with biographical markers and with a bibliography by Hamid Nacer-Khodja, edited by Marie Virolle. This work contains eight unpublished collections of poetry as well as other writings (political texts, testimonies, literary and artistic reviews, correspondence) mostly unpublished.

Visages d'Algérie: Regards sur l'art, Paris, Paris Méditerranée, Alger, EDIF 2000, 2002. Textes rassemblés par Hamid Nacer-Khodja, préface de Guy Dugas.

PUBLISHED ARTICLES

Cited here are only articles not included in other works by/on Sénac.

« Littérature engagée ? Le roman algérien », Alger, *L'Africain*, n° 636, 8 juillet 1946 et n° 641, 7 août 1946.

« Note critique sur Forge », *L'Africain*, Alger, n° 686, 19 juin 1947.

« Un grand écrivain français natif d'Oranie: Albert Camus », *Paris, Casablanca*, n° 208, 8 août 1947.

« Albert Camus », *Oran Républicain*, 30 septembre 1947.

« Notes sur le roman algérien », *Ophrys*, Paris, n° 3, octobre 1947, pp. 152–163.

« Témoignage sur la révolte », *Le Soleil noir/Positions*, Paris, n° 1, février 1952, pp. 90–93.

MISCELLANEOUS

M . . . , Alger, n° 1, avril 1949 (mimeographed).

« Je ne crois pas au chômage mais à la chance » *La Dépêche quotidienne d'Alger*, 3 août 1950.

Soleil, Alger, n° 1, janvier 1950 à n° 7–8, février 1952.

Terrasses, Alger, n° 1, juin 1953.

UNPUBLISHED DOCUMENTS

Journal du sana (Alger-Rivet), 1947–1948.

Le Soleil interdit, Paris, 1954–1958. Tragédie.

Correspondances Sénac-Camus (1947–1958).

Correspondances Sénac-Char (1949–1951).

Correspondances de Sénac avec Suzanne Agnely, Jean Grenier, Jean Paulhan et les
    éditions Gallimard (1951–1959).

« Carnets de Sénac (1954–1967) ».

« Manuscrits d'émissions radiophoniques de Sénac (1949–1967) ».

Miscellaneous drafts, autographed, and handwritten notes of Sénac (1948–1967).

*These documents, partly included in Pour un terre possible, op. cit., were consulted at the
Sénac collection of the Alcazar Library of Marseille and at the National Library of Algeria.
To these we must add the testimonies, both written and oral, of Jean de Maisonseul and
Jacques Miel.*

Albert Camus

WORKS

Théâtre, Récits, Nouvelles, Paris, Gallimard, Bibliothèque de la Pléiade, 1962.

Essais, Paris, Gallimard, Bibliothèque de la Pléiade, 1965.

Carnets I, Paris, Gallimard, collection « Blanche », 1962.

Carnets II, Paris, Gallimard, collection « Blanche », 1964.

Carnets III, Paris, Gallimard, collection « Blanche », 1987.

Albert Camus–Jean Grenier, Correspondance, Paris, Gallimard, collection « Blanche », 1981.

« Réflexions sur le terrorisme » (textes choisis sous la direction de Jacqueline Lévi-
    Valensi), Paris, Nicolas Philippe, 2002.

MISCELLANEOUS

« Entretien avec Gaëtan Picon », *Le Littéraire*, Paris, 10 août 1946.

« Entretien avec Emmanuel Roblès », *Alger Soir*, 15 novembre 1947.

« Lettre au quotidien », *Le Monde*, Paris, 19–20 juillet 1953.

« Sur un billet et une lettre inédits de Albert Camus à André Rosfelder », *Marseille*, revue de la ville de Marseille, n° 120, 1ᵉʳ trimestre 1980, pp. 105–109.

Works on the Authors

On Jean Sénac

STUDIES

Jean Sénac vivant (sous la direction de Jean Déjeux), Paris, Éditions Saint-Germain-des-Prés, collection « Les Cahiers de Poésie 1 », 1981. Essai, témoignages et documents.

Jean-Pierre Péroncel-Hugoz, *Assassinat d'un poète*, suivi de *Heure de mon adolescence*, Marseille, Éditions du Quai/Jeanne Lafitte, 1983, préface de Tahar Ben Jelloun.

Poésie au Sud: Jean Sénac et la nouvelle poésie algérienne d'expression française, Marseille, Archives de la ville de Marseille, 1983.

Le Soleil fraternel: Jean Sénac et la nouvelle poésie algérienne d'expression française, Marseille, éditions du Quai/Jeanne Lafitte, 1985.

Rabah Bélamri, *Jean Sénac, entre désir et douleur*, Alger, OPU, collection « Classiques Maghrébins », 1989.

AWAL, spécial *Jean Sénac*, Paris, n° 10, 1993.

Jamel-Eddine Bencheikh—Christiane Chaulet-Achour, *Jean Sénac: Clandestin des deux rives*, Biarritz-Paris, Atlantica-Séguier, collection « Les colonnes d'Hercule », 1999.

Françoise d'Eaubonne, *La Plume et le bâillon: Violette Leduc, Nicolas Genka, Jean Sénac, trois écrivains face à la censure*, Paris, L'Esprit frappeur, 2000, « Sur Sénac », pp. 103–127.

Émile Temime et Nicole Tuccelli, *Jean Sénac, l'Algérien: Le poète des deux rives*, Paris, éditions Autrement, collection « Littératures », 2003, préface de Jean Daniel.

On Albert Camus

BIOGRAPHIES

Herbert R. Lottman, *Albert Camus*, Paris, Éditions du Seuil, 1978.

Olivier Todd, *Albert Camus: Une vie*, Paris, Gallimard, collection « Vies », 1996.

STUDIES

Madeleine Bouchez, *Les Justes, Albert Camus*, Hatier, collection « Profil d'une œuvre », 1974.

Tayeb Bouguerra, *Le Dit et le non-dit: À propos de l'Algérie et des Algériens chez Camus*, Alger, OPU-ENAL, s.d. (1991).

Jean-Jacques Brochier, *Camus philosophe pour classes terminales*, Paris, Balland, 1979.

Christiane Chaulet-Achour, *Albert Camus, Alger: « L'Étranger »* et autres récits, Biarritz, Atlantica, collection « Les colonnes d'Hercule » 1998.

Laâdi Flici, *Albert Camus ou la crise de la littérature bourgeoise*, Alger, Éditions Universitaires, s.d. (1967).

Jean Grenier, *Albert Camus: Souvenirs*, Paris, Gallimard, collection « Blanche », 1968.

Roger Grenier, *Albert Camus, soleil et ombre*, Paris, Gallimard, collection « Blanche », 1987.

Laurent Mailhot, *Albert Camus ou l'imagination du désert*, Montréal, Les Presses de l'Université de Montréal, 1973.

Emmanuel Mounier, *Malraux, Camus, Sartre, Bernanos*, Paris, Seuil, 1953.

Conor Cruise O'Brien, *Albert Camus*, Paris, Seghers, collection « Les Maîtres Modernes », 1970.

Bernard Pingeaud commente L'Étranger *d'Albert Camus*, Paris, Gallimard, collection « Foliothèque », 1992.

Roger Quilliot, *La Mer et les prisons: Essai sur Albert Camus*, Paris, Gallimard, Hachette, collection « Génies et Réalités », 1964.

Camus et la politique (sous la direction de Jeanyves Guérin), Paris, L'Harmattan, collection « Histoire et Perspectives Méditerranéennes », 1986.

MISCELLANEOUS

Albert Camus (catalogue de l'exposition de l'Université de Nice, 8–14 mai), Aix-en Provence, Édisud, 1981.

Albert Camus (album iconographique), Paris, Gallimard, collection « Bibliothèque de la Pléiade », 1982.

Studies and Articles on the Authors
On Jean Sénac

« La bourse de Lourmarin attribuée à deux jeunes Algériens: S. Galliéro et J. Sénac », *Alger-Républicain*, 2 août 1950.

Critiques de presse sur *Le Soleil sous les armes* par Claude Roy, *Libération*, Paris, 6 mars 1958 et par René Lacôte, *Les Lettres françaises*, Paris, n° 714, 20–26 mars 1958.

Jean Déjeux « Les rencontres de Sidi Madani (Algérie) », *Revue de l'Occident musulman et de la Méditerranée*, Aix-en-Provence, n° 20, 2ème semestre 1975, pp. 165–174. This study came out of the Sénac collection before it was deposited at the National Library of

Algeria.

Jean Déjeux, « La revue algérienne *Soleil* (1950–1952) fondée par Jean Sénac et les revues culturelles de 1937 à 1962 », *Présence francophone*, Sherbrooke, n° 19, automne 1979, pp. 5–28.

On Albert Camus

« Camus l'Algérien », *Simoun*, Oran, n° 32 (numéro spécial), 9ᵉ année, 1960.

Gabriel Audisio, « L'Algérien » in *Hommage à Camus*, Paris, Gallimard, 1967.

Malek Haddad, « Le seul respect que je dois à Camus », Constantine, *El Nasr*, 18 février 1967.

Guy Dugas, « Albert Camus et l'épisode de la trêve civile », *Guerre d'Algérie* magazine, Saint-Cloud, n° 6, novembre–décembre 2002, pp. 40–45.

On Both Authors

Claude Liauzu, « Gabriel Audisio, Albert Camus et Jean Sénac: Entre Algérie française et Algérie musulmane », *Confluences Méditerranée*, Paris, L'Harmattan, n° 33, printemps 2000, pp. 161–171.

Émile Témime, « Camus–Sénac ou la déchirure », in *Montagnes, Méditerranée, Mémoire*, mélange offerts à Philippe Joutard, Éditions Musée Dauphinois–Université de Provence, Aix-en-Provence–Grenoble, 2002, pp. 291–302.

Works and Articles on Algerianism

Alain Calmes, *Le Roman colonial en Algérie avant 1914*, Paris, L'Harmattan, 1984.

Jean Déjeux, « Robert Randau et son "Peuple franco berbère" », *Cahiers de littérature générale et comparée*, spécial « Littérature coloniale », Paris, n° 5, automne 1981, pp. 91–99.

———. « Robert Randau, théoricien du roman colonial, "Le roman colonial 2" », *Itinéraires et Contacts de cultures*, volume n° 12, 1990, Paris, L'Harmattan.

Jean Pomier, *Chronique d'Alger (1910–1957) ou le temps des Algérianistes*, Paris, La Pensée Universelle, 1972.

Paul Siblot, « Pères spirituels et mythes fondateurs de l'Algérianisme, "Le roman colonial 1" », *Itinéraires et Contacts de cultures*, volume n° 7, 1987, Paris, L'Harmattan.

———. « L'Algérianisme, fonction et dysfonction d'une littérature coloniale, "Le roman colonial 2" », *Itinéraires et Contacts de cultures*, volume n° 12, 1990, Paris, L'Harmattan.

Revue algérienne des Sciences juridiques, économiques et politiques, spécial « Roman colonial et idéologie colonialiste en Algérie », Alger, n° 1, mars 1974.

Works and Studies on the Algerian War

Henri Alleg (sous la direction de), *La Guerre d'Algérie*, trois tomes, Paris, Temps Actuels, 1981.

Robert Barrat, *Les Maquis de la liberté: Un journaliste au cœur de la guerre d'Algérie*, Paris-Alger, Éditions Témoignage Chrétien, Entreprise Algérienne de Presse, 1992.

Patrick Eveno et Jean Planchais, *La Guerre d'Algérie*, Paris, La Découverte–Le Monde, 1989, and Alger, Laphomic, 1990.

Benjamin Stora, *Histoire de la Guerre d'Algérie*, Paris, La Découverte, collection « Repères », 1995.

———. *La Gangrène et l'oubli: La mémoire de la guerre d'Algérie*, Paris, La Découverte, collection « Essais », 1998.

Charles-Robert Ageron, « L'évolution de l'opinion publique française face à la guerre d'Algérie », *Revue d'études historiques*, Université d'Alger (Institut d'Histoire), n° 9, 1993, pp. 1–15.

Other Works

Literary Works

René Char, *Œuvres complètes*, Paris, Gallimard, « Bibliothèque de la Pléiade », 1985.

Jean Déjeux, *Littérature maghrébine de langue française*, Sherbrooke, éditions Naaman, 1973.

Malek Haddad, *Les zéros tournent en rond*, précédé de Écoute et je t'appelle, Paris, Maspéro, 1961.

Albert Memmi, *Écrivains francophones du Maghreb*, Paris, Seghers, 1985.

Algérie, un rêve de fraternité (textes présentés et réunis par Guy Dugas), Paris, Omnibus, 1997.

Essays and Testimonials

Jean Daniel, *Le Temps qui reste*, Paris, Stock, 1973.

Laurent Goblot, *Apologie de la censure: Petite histoire de la censure à travers les âges et les régimes*, Rodez, Subervie, 1960.

Amar Ouzegane, *Le Meilleur Combat*, Paris, Julliard, 1962.

Jules Roy, *Mémoires barbares*, Paris, Albin Michel, 1989 (réédition, in *Journal*, 3 volumes, Paris, Albin Michel, 1998–2001).

Benjamin Stora et Zakya Daoud, *Ferhat Abbas*, Paris, Denoël, 1995 et Alger, Casbah Éditions, 1995.

Ahmed Taleb-Ibrahimi, *De la décolonisation à la révolution culturelle*, Alger, SNED, 1973.

———. *Lettres de prison*, Alger, SNED, 1996 et 1977.